Entrepreneurship

Playing
To Win

Entrepreneurship

Playing To Win

GORDON B. BATY

President,
Taplin Business Machines, Inc.
and
Lecturer,
Northeastern University

RESTON PUBLISHING COMPANY, INC.
Reston, Virginia 22090
A Prentice-Hall Company

Library of Congress Cataloging in Publication Data

Baty, Gordon B   1938-
  Entrepreneurship: playing to win.

  Includes bibliographical references.
  1. Entrepreneur.   2. New business enterprises.
I.   Title.
HD69.N3B38   338'.04   74-13215
ISBN 0-87909-253-X

© 1974 by
Gordon B. Baty

10 9 8 7 6 5 4 3 2 1

Printed in the United States of America.

To

ROBERT OAKLUND

*engineer, entrepreneur,
and a very tough guy*

1941–1974

CONTENTS

PREFACE

We are not here to sell a parcel of boilers and vats, but the potentiality of growing rich beyond the dreams of avarice.

✻ SAMUEL JOHNSON ✻
Presiding at the sale of Thule's Brewery, London

This is a book for the entrepreneur and the would-be entrepreneur. It was written in the belief that he or she faces a problem that is somewhat unique relative to other professions: Our society offers no apprenticeship. In other professions, such as law, engineering, or medicine, there exists a formal progression of schooling-to-apprenticeship-to-practice, to equip the initiate with some background and experience before he is asked to accept major responsibilities.

As an entrepreneur, on the other hand, you usually must move from an established larger organization into a new enterprise with nothing even resembling an apprenticeship behind you. Without formal indoctrination, you assume responsibility for management of people, resources, and substantial amounts of other people's money. A substantial gap usually exists between what you have learned and experienced, and what you will be required to know to succeed in your new enterprise. It is the author's hope that this book will help to close that gap.

The book is not intended to be a complete field manual of what-every-young-man-should-know-about-starting-companies. That would be much too long and presumptuous, and, consequently, no busy entrepreneur would read it. For very specialized subjects (e.g., accounting, market research, negotiation) other and better references exist. We have attempted, at the end of most chapters, to list a few of the more generally available of these, ranked in order of usefulness.

Our focus throughout is on the problems of the growth-oriented enterprise, as opposed to the small business (although, of course, many of the same management considerations apply to both). We are interested in the problems of the person who, by exploiting some new technological or marketing principle, is attempting to build a rapid-growth company— a company with the potentiality of national or multi-national marketing, the possibility of exponential growth, and the probability of making its founders millionaires in an interestingly short time period.

This book is not offered as an academic, or even a balanced, study of entrepreneurship. It is written from a definite and pragmatic point of view that, baldly stated, is this: *Neither innovative genius, nor hard work, nor even luck, is in itself a guarantee of corporate success.* Assuming that all of these are present in the new venture in at least trace quantities, the missing catalytic element often seems to be what we might call the "entrepreneurial state of mind." It might be characterized as a degree of tough-mindedness that stops somewhere short of combativeness; a confidence in one's intuitive as well as one's rational faculties; a capacity to think tactically on one's feet, as well as to plan strategically in the business school sense; an attitude that stresses timely action based on sometimes inadequate information, ahead of prolonged factfinding; a mental set stressing integration of many facts into action plans, rather than endless differentiation and analysis. It is an attitude that says, in short: "I didn't just come to play the game—I came to win."

If winning, then, is to be our goal, how shall we define it? The author offers the following provisional definition: *The entrepreneur shall have "won" when he succeeds in bringing his firm to a position where, in order to continue the growth of sales and earnings, a substantial infusion of new capital is required.* This definition by no means implies, of course, that all the perils are behind him. Indeed, many of the most challenging ones lie just ahead. Does he now go public? Sell out to a larger firm? Sell out to a competitor? And how does *he* cash in? When and in what way will he manage to exchange some of his ever-diminishing share of the company for real, spendable money?

Clearly, our definition of "winning" merely assumes that the most basic, elementary business objectives have been met. The business has been born, has survived the perils of infancy, and has been set upon a trajectory of profitable, sustainable growth. From there on, the entrepreneur's problems are of the sort that many businessmen have, or would like to have.

We hope that this book will become a resource for the entrepreneur —to stimulate your thinking, to get you talking to the right sorts of people and reading some useful literature. We hope it will save you some calendar time, some costly mistakes, some needless worry, and some irreplaceable entrepreneurial energy. We hope that it offers the incipient entrepreneur some idea of how to go about collecting his building blocks— and to the functioning entrepreneur, some more glue to hold them all together.

Gordon B. Baty

ACKNOWLEDGMENTS

Were it possible, I would gladly claim credit for all of the ideas contained in this book. However, I can claim only responsibility for the final product, and for acknowledgment of the very helpful direct and indirect contributions of a number of fine people, among whom are:

Herbert Baer, Esq.   Daniel W. Kennedy
Dwight M. Baumann   Richard Morse
William Congolton   V. J. Ryan
Nick DeWolf   Geoff Timmons
Alexander Dingee   David Turner
Brian Haslett   Eric Von Hippel

. . . and others too numerous to mention.

Thanks, too, to Ms Leslie Burke, who prepared the manuscript, and to Fred Easter of Reston Publishing Company, Inc., who served as general cheerleader.

PART I

FORMATION

1

why

start

a

company?

The reasonable man adapts himself to the world, the unreasonable man attempts to adapt the world to himself. Therefore all progress depends upon the unreasonable man.

✻ GEORGE BERNARD SHAW ✻

ENTREPRENEURS—WHAT MAKES THEM TICK?

It should not be astonishing that entrepreneurs have been studied, as individuals and as groups, to a rather extensive degree. Psychologists are interested in finding out what motivates them. Investors are interested in finding some saliva test that will tell them, in advance, which entrepreneurs are going to make them rich. Business school professors have begun to be interested in the questions of whether and how entrepreneurial behavior patterns and skills can be taught. Legions of people in government (as well as their academic consultants) have begun seeking ways to engage entrepreneurs in programs of regional development, minority enterprise, leadership training, export promotion, and "technology transfer"—all in the name of the commonweal.

Needless to say, all of this activity has produced not one, but several disparate literatures on entrepreneurial motivation and behavior. Books have been written, reports filed, symposia convened, theses and learned papers ground out. Some of the more interesting specimens of this genus are listed in the "References" to this chapter, and are recommended reading. From a practical standpoint, however, it does the entrepreneur very little good to know that his statistical chances of success are relatively poor if (a) he is a Gentile; (b) his father was not a businessman or self-employed professional; (c) he has a Ph.D. level education; (d) he does not have three like-minded but complementary colleagues.

5

The germinal question to ask at the outset is somewhat existential: Why should *I* start a company? The range of possible valid answers to this question includes the following:

1 / To make a lot more money than I could with some other application for my energies for a like time.

2 / To get out of a professional rut—to see ideas through to completion, to gain professional recognition, to accept responsibility for the full consequences of my ideas.

3 / To be my own boss, to control my own destiny, to set my own hours, etc.

4 / To prove to myself (my wife, my husband, my father, my ex-boss, etc.) that I can do it.

5 / To advance technology, society, etc.

6 / To develop and deploy talents I feel that I have outside my area of specification.

7 / To show up somebody with whom I intend to compete.

This list could be greatly extended.

None of these rationales is without some subjective validity, and no doubt examples of companies founded on the basis of each could be shown. In real life, however, human motives are never unmixed. Your own answer will be a weighted sum of several of these, plus some additional twists resulting from your own unique outlook and experience. The question is, Does the sum of *all* of these justify the cost, sacrifice, and risk of becoming an entrepreneur? The sum should be reckoned, but the yes–no answer should be held in abeyance, at least until you can more clearly evaluate some of the probable costs. Such evaluation is the subject of the next chapter.

From our list of possible motivations, it may appear that all are of equal merit, since all are of some subjective validity. Nothing could be further from the case. It appears that the most successful firms are started by those who are predominantly motivated by No. 1 in the list, and, to a lesser degree, by No. 2. To the extent that you are concerned with rebelling against your employer, proving yourself to yourself or others, advancing social causes, etc., you are at least statistically allying yourself with less-successful-to-unsuccessful entrepreneurs.

The central objective of the enterprise is to make money for its owners. To the extent that you are seeking to maximize a number of other effects, you will inevitably be diluting your energies from the central objective. When the business dies, *all* objectives are lost. And it will take most of your energy just to keep it alive.

"Why start a company?" is a question that can be answered on yet a different level. During the last decade, a variety of factors had turned many talented and capable young people away from business enterprise as a form of self-fulfillment and social contribution. Charles Reich in *The Greening of America* epitomizes this mentality: We as a people have abandoned Consciousness I (the ruthless entrepreneurial spirit) in favor of Consciousness II (the gray organization man) but through enlightenment we should evolve soon to Consciousness III (the socially concerned man) to achieve the long-awaited Greening.[1] How ironic it must seem to Mr. Reich that significant numbers of talented and educated young people appear to have come full circle, abandoning the beatitudes of Consciousness III for some sense of purpose and accomplishment of socially useful tasks through starting new enterprises—a return, it might seem, to Consciousness I!

Such enterprises are not necessarily trivial (from the economic standpoint) and are often begun by people whose talents range well beyond the making of leather belts or the fixing of bicycles. In the Boston area, some examples of such enterprises include computer dating and roommate matching services, newspaper and book publishing enterprises, health care delivery systems, computerized legal reference systems, computerized medical diagnosis, specialized teaching systems designed for a myriad of clients, ranging from retarded children to immigrant English students with widely varying needs, consulting and hardware firms in pollution abatement. The list could be extended to considerable length.

The significant point is this: There is no inherent conflict between the possession of a social conscience and the possession of entrepreneurial drive. This "conflict" exists principally in the minds of journalists. Moreover, without talented and unique individuals who possess both qualities, little of significant value would be accomplished. Not only are most of our successful businesses started by such people, but these same people also start and operate our clinics, laboratories, universities, and consumer protection agencies—and most of the other new initiatives that contribute to what is popularly considered progress.

This is in no way to say that there are no entrepreneurs motivated by cupidity and greed; nor is it to say that most or even many new enterprises are initiated with the intention, let alone the prospect, of accomplishing any significant social end. However, some successful new enterprises *are* organized to accomplish specific social goals, and there exists

---

[1] Reich, Charles A., *The Greening of America*. New York: Bantam, 1971.

no inherent conflict between such goals and profit. Additionally, social ends are sometimes served even in the absence of conscious social goals. One hears, for example, that the purpose of our society has shifted from the creation of material goods to the creation of jobs. To the extent that even a mundane new enterprise creates jobs, incomes, payroll taxes, human dignity, and reduced welfare costs that might not otherwise develop, it is *inadvertently* playing a very desirable and constructive role in society. A similar case could be made for the creation of desirable goods, desirable services, much-needed exports, etc.

SOME NATURAL ADVANTAGES OF ENTREPRENEURS

There is another set of reasons why more talented and ambitious people should consider entering into a new business enterprise. They are as follows:

1 / *Going into business is not as difficult as is often supposed.* "Sacrifices," while you must be *prepared to* make them, are not always, in fact, *made.* Enormous talent is not necessary. As a matter of fact, it is sometimes a liability. Engineering, sales, and "business" people usually can be hired when needed. There is enough professional help available, on both a part- and full-time basis.

2 / *At no time and in no place on earth have the conditions ever been more propitious for starting a new business.* Hundreds of venture capitalists exist in the United States, in a form all but unknown in other countries. Banks, accounting firms, investment bankers, and other institutions have acquired an understanding of new enterprise that is unmatched at any time or in any place. The whole essence of capitalism and the Protestant Ethic (whether or not you take it neat) is at work, to the benefit of the new enterprise.

3 / *There are hundreds of companies that will design, manufacture, and package your product, to your specifications.* There are inventors, consultants, lawyers, and vendors who will work with you, advise you, sell you their goods and services on very liberal terms—perhaps for stock. Maybe these people hope to develop a major new customer, or, more likely, just to share in the excitement of your venture.

4 / *In the United States innumerable ready-made channels of distribution exist for nearly any class of product.* In an open, mixed economy of our type, there are commission representatives, distributors, wholesalers, house-brand buyers, jobbers of every description—all waiting for the new product that will really "click" for them.

5 / *At no time and in no place have skilled people been so readily accessible to the new enterprise.* There are several reasons for this: (a) At any given moment, many people are dissatisfied with bureaucracy, lack of recognition, and dead-end careers in large firms. They would seriously consider a stimulating, if less secure, position in a small new enterprise. (b) Unlike many other industrial societies, ours does not stigmatize the job-changer. You can hire away the best salesman from your competitor without incurring the moral wrath of the entire community. (c) People are more mobile than ever. It is common practice to recruit for top people across an entire continent—and top people *expect* to move wherever opportunity and growth take them. (d) Due to tax considerations and emotional preferences, many professionals will work as hard for stock as they will for cash. A "piece of the action" is as much in the American tradition as winning the Rose Bowl.

6 / *It is more difficult to fail than is often imagined.* The business failure statistics collected by Dun and Bradstreet and mournfully recited by the press are compilations that include every type of venture from the doomed "Ma and Pa grocery" to moribund street railways, gas stations, small jobbers, wholesalers, needle trades firms, and every other conceivable form of enterprise. When the lugubrious chant about 80 percent business failures starts, tune out. This is data, not information. A more

interesting analysis was put forth by Professor Edward Roberts of MIT, who estimated that only about 20 percent (of the large number) of MIT spinoff firms ever fail completely. And should failure become imminent, the extraordinary bankruptcy laws of our land (discussed in a later chapter) provide still another mechanism to protect the struggling new enterprise.

7 / *In federal and local governments a significant bias toward small business exists.* The declared purpose, of course, is to permit small firms to compete with large firms. The effect, however, is to produce a positive (if not altogether undeserved) bias toward small business. This bias shows itself in the small business set-asides in federal government, in the existence of the Small Business Administration (SBA) and the Small Business Investment Corporations (SBIC), in the existence of a variety of regional development authorities, as well as in other ways. Our entire tax structure, with capital gains, "Subchapter S" corporations, tax-loss carry-forwards and carry-backs, and "Section 1244" corporations, also tends to create a desirable climate in which to raise capital for a new venture. It is debatable how effective these various measures have been in actuality in promoting the small business sector, but surely no one can doubt the *intent* behind such legislation and appropriations.

8 / *The personal and professional risks of a new enterprise are rather less than normally imagined.* To be sure, you may be giving up a $25,000 job for a $10,000 job for a few quarters; you may miss some vacations and some professional meetings. Yet, assuming the worst, you lose your savings and go back to a $25,000 job, having become a broader and more valuable person than you were when you left. None of this is to say that the process is risk-free; nothing worth doing ever is. It merely says that the downside risks are not only unthinkable, but also probably a lot less than you'd imagine.

9 / *Starting a business doesn't require as much experience as you might think.* Naturally, business experience and contacts are usually an asset. However, the person who

goes to work for a large company to get 10 or 15 years of solid experience before starting out on his own is just fooling himself. With a few notable exceptions, most big companies provide the poorest sort of background for the would-be entrepreneur. Most people find themselves working upward through a functional specialty, such as manufacturing, accounting, research, or sales, gaining experience that is negotiable only in that or a similar company. Moreover, experience teaches us our limitations all too well, and makes us pessimistic about the ability of new ideas to get anywhere. Some real-world experience is, of course, essential; more essential, however, is the enthusiastic damn-the-torpedoes spirit that one expects from the young (but that one is sometimes pleasantly surprised to find in the not-so-young). Enthusiasm, vigor, energy, and the skin of a rhinoceros are far more valuable assets than the "many years of experience," which are all too often the same year repeated many times.

10 / Finally, we reach the consideration that is probably more significant than the rest together: Starting a new business is more fun than almost anything else. Of course, you're going to have to work long hours. But any professional worth his salt, no matter what his field, works long hours. Nights, weekends, holidays—60 and 70 hour weeks. Of course, there are going to be headaches—and maybe stomach aches, too. But how do you expect to avoid them in any other significant professional job? The big difference is this: Instead of immersing yourself in someone else's organization and struggling with its problems, in a new enterprise you create your own organization (with its own problems), and run it as you think it should be run. You stand or fall on the result. And that's about as much fun as most of us can handle.

Perhaps at this juncture, we can step back from the question "Why start a new company?" and turn it around: "Why *not* start a new company?" The remaining chapters of this book are dedicated to those inclined to say, "Let's get on with it!"

REFERENCES

1 / McClelland, D.C., *The Achieving Society*. New York: D. Van Nostrand Co., 1961.

This is the classic, a fascinating study of entrepreneurs and what makes them tick.

2 / McClelland, D.C., "**Achievement Motivation Can Be Developed**," *Harvard Business Review*, November–December 1965.

Discusses the philosophy, methods, and limitations of efforts to develop entrepreneurial drive.

3 / Mancuso, Joseph, *Fun and Guts: The Entrepreneur's Philosophy*. Reading, Mass.: Addison-Wesley Co., 1973.

This is an amusing and generally accurate account of the stages an entrepreneur goes though in building a company.

4 / Collins, O. F., and D. G. Moore, *The Enterprising Man*. E. Lansing, Mich.: Michigan State University Business Studies, 1964.

This is a unique work, in which 100 entrepreneurs from all different types of industries were studied with regard to personality traits. Entrepreneurs turn out to be a rather grubby, asocial, outcast, and generally unlikeable bunch. The book even includes a sort of psychoanalysis of the typical entrepreneurial type, examining his childhood deprivations, etc. "Nice guys don't win" is the message.

5 / Roberts, E. B., "**How To Succeed in a New Technology Enterprise**," *Technology Review*, December 1970.

All you need are the right parents, the right age, the right religion, etc, etc. Based on studies of about 300 MIT spinoff technology ventures.

6 / Roberts, E. B., "**Entrepreneurship and Technology**", *Research Management*, XI, No. 4 (1968).

Discusses the influence of various factors on technology transfer and, indirectly, on entrepreneurial success. Centers on the role of the entrepreneur.

7 / Myers, Gustavus, *History of the Great American Fortunes*. New York: Modern Library, reprint of 1907 ed.

If you really *want to know how the old rich got that way, read this first-rate bit of muckraking, written before Nader's grandfather was born.*

8 /   U.S., Congress, Select Committee on Small Business, **Small Business Investment Act.** 88th Cong., 1st sess., 1963.

Interesting insights into the Congress' position on small business in general.

2

risks
and
rewards

It is only by risking our persons from one hour to another that we live at all.

* WILLIAM JAMES *

The decision to become an entrepreneur has two basic components: (a) Am I an entrepreneur? Do I have the abilities, the attitudes, the motivation? And (b) Are the potential rewards commensurate with the risks? Each of these questions has a number of components that should be explored before any decision is reached. The world is full of examples of successful and wealthy entrepreneurs. (Indeed, it is difficult to find examples of first-generation wealth made by men *not* in business for themselves.) In accounts of their experiences, however, one seldom gets an accurate picture of the risks that confronted them or how they evaluated these risks at the outset. It is questionable as to whether these people even *recognized* the risks when they started their businesses.

It all looks too easy. The unsuccessful entrepreneurs are less obvious. They are hard to identify since they don't advertise much and often give self-serving accounts of the failure mode (e.g., "Our product was too advanced for its time", "We did not have enough capital", etc.).

It is even more difficult to evaluate the risks taken by the unsuccessful entrepreneur, and thus to profit from his experience. About the best one can do is to evaluate one's own risks, in the light of one's own situation, and go from there.

FINANCIAL RISKS

Usually the financial risks involved in starting a new enterprise are numerically low, but of great importance to the entrepreneur. They involve his savings (his house equity, perhaps) and maybe some temporary reduction in his salary. Many people are unwilling to even consider a reduction in their standard of living or in their financial security in order to start a new company. They are not entrepreneurs at heart.

However—and here is the crucial point—while you must be *prepared* to make financial sacrifices, there is a very good chance that you will never actually *have* to *make* them. It is much more important to *appear* willing to put your hand in the fire.

To illustrate—several years ago a young man in Massachusetts decided to start a company in specialty food packaging. His personal assets consisted of equity in a house, the cash value of his insurance, and a few thousand dollars in savings. When the time came, at last, to leave his job with a food broker and set out on his own, he sat down with his boss and showed him the business plan. The boss, himself an entrepreneur, was impressed by the idea. He was, however, more impressed by the fact that the young man's business plan involved many months of deferred salary, as well as most of his savings and a second mortgage on his house. This guy had to be crazy, the boss thought, or else onto a sure bet. He decided it was the latter and volunteered the necessary seed money in exchange for a minority equity position. As a result, both made a great deal of money, and a successful, growing company exists today. *Note:* Our entrepreneur never missed a paycheck, never refinanced his house, and never put over 25 percent of his savings into the venture!

So, when considering the financial risks, remember:

1 / The *real* risks may be less than the *apparent* risks.

2 / You can always get another job if the company folds.

3 / You can rebuild your savings account.

4 / Corporation law prevents your being liable for more than you have in the company.

Think it over.

CAREER RISKS

This is an important area that is seldom discussed by business writers. Yet, it may be even more significant than the financial risks encountered in a new enterprise. Simply stated, it is the risk that, having stepped outside your profession for a few years, re-entry may be difficult. Certain professions, such as law, are structured to permit an interruption in one's career for a few years without excessive penalty. This is one reason why so many politicians and public servants are lawyers. Some other professional careers are not as easily turned off and on at will, however. A professor, leaving his post, may miss an opportunity to ever achieve tenure. A scientist starting a small company may discover that the demands on his time are so heavy that he loses touch with his colleagues, his funding sources, and the broader front of research progress in his field. A very senior executive may relinquish seniority, vested savings, stock options, or retirement benefits earned. A skilled machinist may relinquish seniority in his union (a nice thing to have when layoffs hit).

However, there is another side to the story. A take-charge person who has evidenced the courage to leave and start his own business, even if he in turn leaves *that* business, returns to his old role as a broader, tougher person. (At least some organizations seem to believe this—and if your old one doesn't, its competitor probably will.) Moreover, those who start new companies are probably more inclined than others to find new and different uses for their training, and thus are among the least likely candidates to sit wondering if their old desk is still waiting empty at Titanic Industries.

PERSONAL RISKS

The level of personal risk is the most difficult of all to analyze. It is difficult because it involves one's own family members, social friends, and other human beings whose reactions may be harder to predict than one's own. Unlike financial cost, which may be avoided under some circumstances, the commitment of almost all one's leisure time and energies is all-but-inescapable in starting a new company. Many marriages simply cannot survive the long absences of one member from hearth and home. Vacations have a way of getting postponed indefinitely. Meals get cold or go unprepared. Weekend outings vanish from the calendar. Social invitations go unaccepted and unrepeated. Reduced family cash flow may dictate fewer dinners out, less entertaining, etc. These factors put a strain upon any household. Whether they might wrench *yours* is a question that deserves some sober reflection.

On the asset side, however, are the following considerations:

1 / Your absence from the hearth may create the opportunity for your wife's going back to work full- or part-time, or for your husband's doing some work around the house. This may be the best thing to happen, not only to your spouse but also to your marriage.

2 / The necessity of constant absence from home diminishes with time. (Let your new sales manager make some of those trips to Cincinnati. Let your accountant prepare those draft budgets for your review. Let your bright young assistant deliver that paper at the Association meeting.) Eventually, you will be able to find more time to devote to your domestic life.

3 / You must ask yourself what the future time demands of your present job are going to be, if you are to be successful. Many managers, as they scale the corporate ladder, find that their broadened responsibilities keep them away from home more, rather than less. The reasons are many: attending meetings with a far away subsidiary, troubleshooting for the new plant in Brussels, attending sales meetings and "executive development" sessions, and expanding one's social and civic responsibilities to fit the perceived desires of the firm—all at the expense of one's private life. The important thing is to compare your future life as an entrepreneur with your *future* life on your present trajectory.

In summary, of all the risks (those to your financial situation, career, and personal life) the last usually proves to be the most important—primarily because the costs are the least escapable, and secondly because its total impact is the hardest to predict. A demolished home life is a high price to pay for business success, and can ultimately undermine the company itself.

Here are some ways in which entrepreneurs have dealt with this problem:

1 / Set aside a sacred day—Sunday is usually best—and make it an inviolable rule always to be home and never

to schedule work or meetings. This is harder than it sounds.

2 / Make sure you remember social engagements, your spouse's and your kids' birthdays, anniversaries, etc., so that something happens, even if you're not home.

3 / Substitute the 3-day weekend for vacations. Four or five short trips a year will go far in refreshing mind and spirit if time and finances don't permit a regular vacation.

4 / Occasionally, conduct business over breakfast, and meet your husband or wife in town for lunch.

5 / Put your spouse to work on specific company problems as his or her time and/or interests permit. If feasible, involve them in a full- or part-time professional capacity, as a partner, employee, or consultant. In addition to helping, they will gain insights into your problems, and a sense of sharing in the venture. But be sure the company pays the going rate for this help—even if it means giving IOUs!

6 / Keep your spouse informed, thus sharing your hopes and problems and not shutting your family out of your big adventure. Don't hesitate to use your spouse as a sounding board when you're thinking aloud about a problem.

This list is comprised only of suggestions. You can imagine at least a dozen more ways in which to ease the strain upon your domestic life—and perhaps turn your venture into something of an adventure for your family, as well as for yourself.

REWARDS

The rewards of being a successful entrepreneur are legendary. There are few other ways in which wealth can be accumulated in this age, and fewer still that provide the sort of satisfactions that can come from the use of all of one's talents and energies in building a successful company of one's own. In a society such as ours, that exalts commercial success above inherited status, cultural attainments, or even intellectual accomplishment, a winning entrepreneur is probably assured a disproportionately high return on his investment of energy, time, and worry, relative to other equally talented, hard-working people.

An anonymous sage once observed, "Money isn't everything, but it's sure better than whatever's in second place." Among the second-place contenders, excluding things that money can buy, we must list a sense of social contribution, professional satisfaction, community status, and perhaps even a sense of power. Sometimes even "not-too-successful" companies provide these rewards to their founders in substantial degrees.

HOW TO TELL IF YOU'RE AN ENTREPRENEUR

You're an entrepreneur if—

1 / Your analysis of risk and reward shows that the probable gains outweigh the probable net costs by a substantial margin, and,

2 / Your personal profile is not outrageously at odds with the known facts about successful entrepreneurs (see Chapter 1, "References").

CONVENTIONAL WISDOM ⬅ ➡ **REALITY**

The risks and costs of failure are almost unthinkably high for a person starting a new company today.

Not only are the risks much less than commonly assumed, but also by the use of some planning, they can often be reduced further, if not altogether eliminated. Your financial backers may be taking a lot more risk than you are.

REFERENCES

1 / McClelland, D.C., "**Entrepreneurs Are Made—Not Born**", *Forbes*, June 1, 1969.

This is a painless capsule of McClelland's ideas on motivation in general. Message: *Money does not motivate people (!)*

2 / Hoad, W. M., and P. Rosko, *Management Factors Contributing to Success or Failure of New Small Manufacturers.* Ann Arbor, Mich.: University of Michigan, Bureau of Business Research, 1964.

This study demonstrates the various risk elements of start-up, with a sample of 100 companies.

3 / Rubenstein, A. H., *Problems of Financing and Managing New Research-Based Enterprises in New England.* Boston: Federal Reserve Bank of Boston, 1958.

This is an early but still relevant study of the risks and problems of technology entrepreneurs.

4 / "**How the High Fliers Take Off**", *Business Week*, November 22, 1962, 112–116.

Some wild case histories from the zenith of the 1962 bull market (e.g., Cogar Technology).

5 / Allen, Louis L., *Starting and Succeeding in Your Own Small Business.* New York: Grosset and Dunlap, 1968.

6 / Mayer, K. B., *The First Two Years: Problems of Small Firm Growth and Survival,* Washington, D.C.: Small Business Administration, 1961.

7 / Landen, C. W., *et al, A Study of the Problems of Small Electronics Manufacturing Companies in Southern California.* San Diego, Calif.: San Diego College, Bureau of Business and Economic Research, 1962.

3

what
kind
of
company?

Sometimes I only find out where I should be going by going somewhere I don't want to be.

✽ BUCKMINSTER FULLER ✽

A very fundamental distinction, one understood by very few new entrepreneurs, exists between two types of companies: (a) those companies organized to profit from the sale of products, and (b) those organized to profit from the sale of stock. To draw this distinction is not to say that the two are necessarily mutually exclusive—they aren't. However, some companies with excellent earnings may not sell for much (i.e., for a low price–earnings ratio), while other companies with negligible earnings or even large losses may sell for a lot of money (i.e., infinite or negative price–earnings). The reasons are not hard to understand. A company with good earnings may sell cheaply because:

1 / It is in a static or declining industry.

2 / Impending events, such as patent expirations, growing competition, and antitrust actions, may cloud the future.

3 / Its growth is limited by its local character (e.g., a dry cleaning plant), a saturated market, scarcity of raw material (e.g., fish processing), etc.

4 / Its product or technology may be simply out of style in the investment community (e.g., computer software firms and nursing home chains, as of time of writing). Brokerage house customers may just have lost a bundle in similar companies.

Conversely, a company with terrible earnings may sell for a lot of money because:

1 / It owns substantial net assets (i.e., high liquidation value).

2 / It has a tax-loss status of value to the buyer.

3 / It has a product or service that has tremendous potential.

4 / It is in style.

The trick in deciding what kind of company you're going to start lies, of course, in finding a combination that will make money from product sales *and* from equity sales. Elementary, you say. But, as experience will verify, it is much harder to actually make money in a rapidly growing firm than is generally supposed. It is incredible how rising materials costs, expanding sales organizations, product redesign, product delays, and collection problems can devour that marvelous projected gross margin. The obvious hedge is this: Make every conceivable effort to be in one of the areas in which companies with less-than-zero earnings can be sold profitably, *or* be in a dead-end situation where the profits that can be milked are so great that you don't care if you have to throw your stock away in five years. Above all, don't get caught in the middle of the intervening spectrum. As a matter of practical experience, it is probably true that the stylish company is the better choice for the first-time entrepreneur, while the special-situation or liquidation type deal is the province for more experienced heads.

Most entrepreneurs like to think in terms of building a company that can eventually go public, thus allowing them to cash out via the founders' stock. It is obviously true that many successful companies are acquired by bigger companies, and some can be said to have been developed and groomed with that disposition in mind.

A third (if somewhat dated) philosophy is to build a solid company to own, operate, and pass on to one's children. There is nothing wrong with that. However, generally speaking, if you build a company that meets the tests of the capital markets in order to go public, the chances are that either of the other two routes will still be open to you, should you change your mind. The reverse of this statement is generally not true.

SERVICE VS. MANUFACTURING

It may be that there once was a bias within the capital markets toward companies whose product was hardware rather than services. It is apparent, however, that today an innovative idea in service or in service delivery can be quite capable of attracting both capital and investor interest. A roster of currently stylish company areas would include examples of both types of company. Service industries that have attracted investor interest in the last few years include computer time-sharing, health service delivery (e.g., nursing homes), medical monitoring, fast food merchandising, campground franchising, tax preparation services, and mutual funds. In the gradual shift of our economy toward more service industries, entrepreneurs and investors alike should become increasingly sophisticated in judging the risks and returns of new service ventures. Both hardware and software offer opportunity for the entrepreneur with an innovative product to market.

FASHIONS IN TECHNOLOGIES AND MARKETS

Although it is true that definite fashion trends may be found in capital markets, it is a bit unfair to use the word "fashion" when referring to the venture capitalist—unfair in that it connotes an irrational preoccupation with trivia (e.g., hemlines and lapel widths). In fact, most venture capitalists and "special-situation men" in brokerage houses are engaged in a rational, cold-blooded analysis of what they can *sell*.

Changing fashions come about in new ventures not because someone wants to make the shares of stock that his customer purchased last year obsolete, but because new and exciting ideas and technologies are constantly being created. Innovative marketing ideas are emerging, and new market needs are developing. At the same time, as the glamour industries of yesterday mature and consolidate, competition reduces opportunities for large profits, and fewer new ventures come forth for capital from those industries. Moreover, it is invariably the case that some new technologies (e.g., cryogenics) and some new markets (e.g., the "Youth Market") are oversold, yield disappointing returns to their early investors, and are pushed aside in the venture capital market in the next wave of changing fashions. For these and other reasons, discernible trends do exist in the market. It is up to the pragmatic entrepreneur to discern them.

The best way to discover the current trend is to find out what's being financed. A look at the annual reports of some of the major public venture capital firms will indicate what kinds of businesses have been added to and deleted from their portfolios. Conversations with management of some of the not-so-public ones can often yield similar information. One of the most useful sources of such data is the *OTC Market Chronicle*, published weekly, which gives summary information on most new ventures presently in registration with the SEC, as well as rundowns on the product and stock performance of many over-the-counter companies. A still better source, if you can get your hands on it, is the monthly *SBIC/Venture Capital*, published by Stanley Reubel and Associates, Chicago. Reading such a publication over a period of time can also give you a very good sense of the investment patterns of different financial institutions and underwriters. One, for example, may specialize in community antenna TV companies, while another seems to follow medical electronics firms, and so on. The reason for this pattern of specialization is fairly obvious: A firm simply gains experience in evaluating ideas and entrepreneurs of a particular sort, thereby reducing both cost and risk.

Once you have tentatively identified your general area of interest or have confirmed that your initial idea is sufficiently fashionable, you would do well to approach whatever underwriters are active in that area and have a long talk with them. You'll learn a great deal about who the present and future leaders are in your particular field, and what's going on in the industry; and you will get at least some idea of how much longer that industry will stay in the "Top Ten." The editors of the industry magazines are another good source of this sort of information. It is their business to be alert to new trends and to evaluate the viability of new developments. They are generally interesting, interested people, and such acquaintances can be extremely valuable to you in terms of publicity and contacts, once your business is off the ground. Take an editor to lunch today. Or better yet, an editor *and* a broker. To paraphrase a tired cliché, "If you're going to sell steak, just be damned sure it's still *sizzling*."

WHERE TO LOOK FOR IDEAS

Despite a very pervasive myth to the contrary, most new companies are *not* started on the basis of new or original ideas. Most are simply based on old ideas that have been updated; current ideas that have been repackaged for a new market; straightforward extensions of existing products; products that are designed to fit into a niche between existing larger competitors, etc. This is one of the reasons why ordinary people can start extraordinarily successful businesses. It is not necessary to be an innovative genius to come up with a suitable idea. Many of the most profitable, and hence fundable, low risk ventures are merely mundane-looking extensions of existing products (e.g., a cheaper hand-held calculator, a higher-performance servo motor, a fancier motor home). One of the best places to look for specific first-product ideas is right under your nose: in the development direction of product lines already being marketed in your target area.

What is required? What will sell? What will the market demand *next* year? This approach may pit you against established competition, but at least you don't have the enormous investment and lead time required for the development of a new market. Investors look with favor upon this approach.

Here are some of the other idea sources that you might also look into, in rough order of descending effectiveness:

Present job environment
Successful entrepreneurs
Trade shows
Trade publications
Editors
Commerce Business Daily
Management consultants
Idea brokers and patent brokers
Venture capital firms
Technology transfer agencies
Regional development agencies
Official Gazette, U.S. Patent Office

Once you have picked a general product there are, of course, many ways in which to focus more closely upon alternative design approaches, existing and abandoned states of the art, probable research efforts by competitors, etc. Agencies such as the Library of Congress National Referral Center, the Smithsonian Institution's Science Information Exchange, and the National Technical Information Service of the United States Department of Commerce are good places in which to find specific information, but aren't much good for browsing.

Once you get into your idea search, you may find that are many people with ideas that seem better than yours—ideas just sitting there, waiting for the right person to match them up with the people and resources needed to exploit them. So don't lock yourself in a closet and try to think of the ideal product. It's probably sitting out there in the world, just waiting for you.

CRITERIA FOR FIRST PRODUCTS

It is important to remember that the product that is one firm's success is another firm's dog. Success and failure are determined by the nature of the organization and the people who will exploit the product. The criteria for a beginning company's first product are particularly stringent, due to the company's extreme limitations in terms of staff, experience, market contact, capital, and every other factor needed to make a new product sell.

The following table offers one general way of classifying your new-product candidates, with illustrative examples.

	Existing product	*Modification of existing product*	*Totally new product*
Existing market	"New" shaving cream	Disposable hospital bedding	Laser surgical instruments
Identifiable market	Pet cosmetics	Hand-held calculators for consumer use	Aerosol cheese spread
Unknown market	One-man submarines	Home video tape systems	Internal combustion pogo stick

Where your first product falls is largely a function of your imagination and/or merit of the product idea itself. However, some generalization is possible.

1 / The closer you are to the northwest corner, the safer and easier to finance your product will be. This is often a winning combination for the first product, even though the potential payoff may be higher for future products.

2 / The further toward the southeast corner you get, the harder it will be to find financing and develop a profitable enterprise.

3 / In general, a new company is better off in the northeast corner, where the market is at least *known*, than in the southwest where you may never make the first sale. This is true because new companies invariably have much less marketing competence than they have product development ability.

4 / Since high rates of return invariably involve higher risk, you ought to consider reserving riskier, higher potential ideas for second or third products. By then you'll have a company going and (hopefully) some modest first-product results.

Here are some of the additional criteria to which the first-product candidates must be subjected:

---

1 / *Is it proprietary?* *This is the first question an investor will ask. It doesn't have to be patented (although patents are great window-dressing), but it should be sufficiently proprietary to permit a long headstart against competitors and a period of extraordinary profits early in the venture to offset start-up costs.*

2 / *Are the initial production costs realistic?* *If your first product is plastic canoes, perhaps they are. If it is sea-going LPG tankers, perhaps they aren't.*

3 / *Are the initial marketing costs realistic?* *A specialized scientific instrument may, measured in this way, be a better first product than a new razor.*

4 / *Does your product have potential for very high gross margins?* *This is almost a necessity for a fledgling company. By this measure, a "new" cosmetic product might be less of a risk than a new machine tool. Note that gross margin is one thing that the financial community really understands.*

5 / *Is the time required to get to market and break even realistic?* *If you have no idea how long it will take to get there, then you can't even estimate how much money you'll need. In most cases, the faster the better. You can always hold your new product in reserve, announcing it*

to the stockholders immediately after you announce your
first profitable quarter.

6 / Is the potential market enormous? By potential market,
look ahead three to five years. By this gage, specialized
instrumentation for student laboratories might be a better
product than specialized instrumentation for metallurgi-
cal laboratories.

7 / Is your product the first member of a growing family?
If so, it's a better first product than a solo virtuoso. If it
requires a lot of high margin accessories or supplies, so
much the better. Most of the best growth companies have
products with large doses of this characteristic. Again,
due to the enormous costs, delays, and uncertainties of
market development, producing a stream of products for
the same market is a safer investment than trying to develop entirely new markets for your old product.

8 / Do you have some ready-made initial customers? It is
certainly impressive to financial backers when you can
list your first ten customers by name.

9 / Are the development cost and calendar time realistic?
Preferably, they are zero. A ready-to-go product, with the
development already paid for (by your old company, the
government, an offshore manufacturer, or anybody else),
gives you a big leg up over other small companies that
dissipate their initial stake in seemingly endless product
development. Save your jazzy product development efforts for your second, third, or fourth product.

10 / Are you in a growing industry? This is not absolutely
essential if the profits and company growth are there, but
there's less room for mistakes. A growing company in a
growing market can survive a lot more management blun-
ders and bad luck and still succeed.

**11 / Can your product and the need for it be understood by
the financial community?** If the product is super-tech-
nical, they can always get a consultant in to evaluate its
merits. But if they can "evaluate" it themselves, you're
golden. One of the best products that I ever saw in this
respect was a tiny, portable, heart-monitoring system for
post-coronary monitoring. Half the people who heard the
presentation had already had coronaries!

The list of criteria could be extended *ad nauseum,* but by now you have the idea of what kinds of questions to ask. If you can answer "yes" to at least six of these eleven, go see your Aunt Hattie about some start-up money. If you ace all eleven, go see Goldman, Sachs.

REFERENCES

1 / Karger, D. W., and R. G. Murdick, *New Product Venture Management.* New York: Gordon and Breach, 1972.

This is the best all-around book on new product development going. It starts with evaluation of market needs and goes right through to public offering. The section on marketing and promotion is particularly good.

2 / Smith, N. R., *Entrepreneur and His Firm; The Relationship Between Type of Man and Type of Company.* East Lansing, Mich.: Michigan State University, Bureau of Business and Economic Research, 1967.

3 / Karger, D. W., and A. B. Jack, *Problems of Small Business in Developing and Exploiting New Products.* Troy, N.Y.: Rensselaer Polytechnic Institute, 1963.

This is the proceedings of a conference on this subject. It includes some very interesting papers on why products run into problems. Excellent bibliography.

4 / Cooper, A. C., "**Entrepreneurial Environment**", *Industrial Research,* September 1970.

Summarizes a study done on the impact of location on success or failure of new enterprises. Study focuses on the electronics industry in Palo Alto, and concludes that there is a right place as well as a right time to start a firm.

5 / The Conference Board Inc., **Generating New-Product Ideas.** CB Report No. 546. New York: The Conference Board Inc., 1972.

A very pragmatic booklet on practical approaches, with references, checklists, sources, and sample company policies.

6 / "**A Checklist for New Industrial Products**", *Journal of Marketing,* July 1959. 70–73.

7 / *Growth and Acquisition Guide—1971 Yearbook.* Cleveland, Ohio: Predicasts Inc., 1972.

Section 1 of this book, "New and Growth Products", gives many excellent ideas on emerging industries, as of 1972.

4

measuring
the
need

Market demand for a product *is the total* volume *that would be bought by a defined* customer group *in a defined* geographical area *in a defined* time period *under a defined* marketing program.

✻ PHILIP KOTLER ✻

It is verifiably true that entrepreneurs are usually worse at selling their own products than they are in any other area of endeavor within the business structure. Yet selling is the most *critical* area of activity in most companies. Its importance cannot be overemphasized, especially in the case of a new venture.

There are many ways of obtaining a product to sell: It can be designed, manufactured to order, imported, or assembled. The one thing that you *yourself* must do is sell it. Your merchandising methods may, in some cases, be the major "product" of your company (*e.g.* Colonel Sanders, Avon, Savings Bank Life Insurance).

Finally, a poor or unrealistic marketing program is one of the major "weak spots" which prospective investors watch out for. This chapter attempts to enumerate some of the major pitfalls present in the planning and execution of a market analysis program, so that you can, with luck, avoid them.

WHAT MARKET RESEARCH IS—AND ISN'T

When you begin to develop a marketing program, the first step is the identification, measurement, and documentation of the *need* for your *product*. The focus placed upon *need* and *product* is intentional.

Much of what passes for "market research" is actually generalized investigation of massive "markets". It is made up of guesses as to the share of the market that can be captured and projections, not backed up by solid figures, of potential growth rates. This kind of cursory approach impresses no one, and never really reaches the important, factual issues with which you will have to deal. Following are some questions which you should ask yourself:

1 / Will you be serving your customers' real needs? What are these needs? How much will your customers be willing to spend for your product? What is different about your product that will cause customers to choose it over that of your competitor?

2 / To what industry will your sales efforts be directed? What is its size now, and at what rate is it growing? Who will your principal customers be? For what purposes will they use your product? How significant a competitor can you be in your industry?

3 / How are selling and distribution usually handled by your competitors? What are the buying habits of your prospective customers? What will selling and distribution cost?

4 / How many industries can you serve? Some entrepreneurs see so many potential applications for their product that they are unable to focus their initial energies upon developing one major class of customer. They try to reach all classes simultaneously, possibly with different distribution methods needed for each class. The results of such a practice can be disastrous!

5 / What are the principal market segments that are reachable, and upon which one will you concentrate? (For example, if you're selling electronic controls to machine tool builders, you will want to concentrate your sales efforts upon those companies that do not have in-house electronics capability.) Who will the principal customers be within your chosen segment? How much will each customer buy? At what price? What product that your customer is presently using will be replaced by your product? What is the competitive product's cost? What will it cost the customer in terms of design change, tooling costs, changes in methods, etc., to switch to your

*product? What market segments, and in what order, do
you wish to reach later on in your endeavor?*

6 / *What are the major representative, distributor, and
dealer firms within the industry that now call on your
prospective customers? Which ones would be most suitable for you to use in your sales effort?*

7 / *Who are your present competitors? Who will they be in
three years? What are the major characteristics of their
products, their marketing methods, and the strengths and
weaknesses of each? Are they planning the introduction
of a new product in the near future that would en-
danger your business? How large and how profitable
are they? Are they making any money* **in areas which
would compete with yours?**

8 / *What will it cost you to sell to your proposed market
segment over the next few years? How much money
should you allocate for such things as salesmen's salaries,
regional office expenses, representatives' commissions,
field service organizations, applications engineering, customer training, warranty repairs, documentation, advertising, and promotion?*

9 / *How long will it take to get your sales effort into full
swing? Will there be a long cycle of need evaluation,
funds approval, and vendor selection? Is a long period of
training on a unique new product required? Is intensive
advertising over long periods of time necessary?*

10 / *What are the names of the ten major customers who
will be buying your product?* (**Note:** *General Electric
Company is not a customer—Joe Snodgrass, equipment
buyer for the General Electric Missile and Toaster Division, Houston Operations, may be.*)

The final distillate of this information-gathering process is the top
line of your *pro forma* profit and loss statement: dollar shipments per
month. This is the great leap, the key assumption, the base of your entire
business plan, the yardstick against which you and your business will be
measured.

In general, it is easier to explain away the absence of profits than
the absence of sales. If sales are materializing on schedule, investors tend

to be more patient about profits that are below your stated target. Therefore, your chances of successfully financing and operating your business are increased by your knowing as much as possible about your product's users and by your ability to present documented evidence regarding your market.

WHERE DO YOU LOOK FOR INFORMATION?

Once you have a business opportunity for which there appears to be good potential, your immediate aim should be researching and documenting that opportunity. In this way you will be able to convince others, as well as yourself, of its validity. There are many sources of data for any new product.

Your first task in the research process will be listing those sources that you will investigate, in their order of use to you. Some data sources, such as direct mail surveys, take a long time to complete and therefore should be begun at once. Others, such as searches of literature, telephone interviews, and personal interviews, will produce almost immediate results and therefore can be pursued at your leisure. In order to make the best use of your time, it is advisable to schedule them around other activities.

Some forms of research, such as library research, can be accomplished with little or no cost to you; others, such as hiring Dun and Bradstreet to analyze their market data base for you, are so costly that you may rule them out altogether. It is important to be sure that you proceed by exhausting those sources that will be least costly and most helpful at the outset of your research.

Some of the most common sources of information on potential markets for new products are discussed below, in approximate order of descending cost-effectiveness.

✠ LIBRARY RESEARCH

This can be initiated in a university or large public library, and can be extended into technically oriented libraries or to the Library of Congress, National Technical Clearing-House, etc. You will make use of all the conventional methods and reference materials used in library research—abstracting services, specialized bibliographies, *Readers' Guide to Periodicals*, technical digest services, and, in some libraries, computer data-retrieval services.

Your research tools will, to a large extent, depend upon the field that you are researching. For example, if you were interested in a use for integrated circuits in automobiles, you could include such references as the electronics trade press and the end-user press (*e.g., Road and Track*); government automotive research standards, and perhaps patent documentation, might also be useful to you.

If this form of research sounds endless to you, you might consider engaging a diligent graduate student to aid in conducting the actual library research, under your close supervision.

✠ QUESTIONNAIRE SURVEYS

The questionnaire survey is the mainstay of market research, whether it is conducted by mail, telephone, or personal interview. You are reaching your prospective customer *directly*, learning about his needs, problems, quantity requirements, and opinions regarding your proposed product. No form of indirect or inferential information is as up to date, helpful to you, or convincing to others. The questionnaire is always used (even if it's memorized) to ensure that the results are as comparable as possible.

There are perils, of course. A poorly structured questionnaire or an interview conducted with a weak format can result in false and/or misleading information. It is difficult, for example, for a customer to estimate his use of a product that he has never seen, that may be the first of its kind, and that is possibly still nonexistent. Books have been written on survey techniques, questionnaire design, and interview psychology. By consulting one or more of these references, you may be able to avoid some of these perils.

✠ EXISTING RESEARCH REPORTS

If the industry that you wish to reach is growing, it has probably been studied by someone in the fairly recent past. The problem is discovering who has done it and where to find the study. Many investment banking firms do such reports, or have them done by consultants for limited distribution to their customers. Various investment advisory services, such as Arthur D. Little's Service to Investors, do much the same thing. Consulting firms' livelihoods depend upon private studies of products and markets, both those that are potential in nature and those that already exist. It is difficult, however, to obtain these reports unless you are in some way connected with the firm that commissioned them.

Some large studies, however, are syndicated by research firms, as well as other agencies, such as Stanford Research Institute or Battelle Memorial Institute. In such studies, which are directed toward many different clients, many copies may be available and your chances of obtaining one are better. In order to find out if any current study or report exists, ask your prospective customers, prospective competitors, and trade association personnel.

✠ PUBLISHED MARKET STATISTICS

There are two important sources of published market statistics: the United States Department of Commerce and trade associations. The economic time series of the USDC is often criticized because of the tendency toward aggregation of figures, as well as slow reporting, smallness of samples, and out-of-date SIC classifications. However, in some industries you will find the data to be quite current and detailed. Moreover, you can always contact the USDC directly, and tell them what information you need. They have much data at their disposal (some already published and some not), and they may be able to provide you with information that is more detailed and current than you would expect. There may be a charge, or they may do it for free, depending upon the complexity of your needs.

Trade associations usually publish gross industry sales, which are broken down into major product categories. Get in touch with those associations relevant to you, and find out what they publish. If you are able to get to know someone on their staff at a national level, you may be able to obtain the information that they have, but don't publish. Such information is not necessarily secret, but may simply not be in demand. Your ultimate objective, of course, is to find out who is shipping how much to whom, and to find such information may require some persistence on your part.

✠ TRADE ASSOCIATION MEETINGS AND TRADE SHOWS

It is possible to obtain a lot of valuable information by attending the appropriate annual meetings or trade shows. You'll find out who your liveliest competitors and customers are, who is spending the most money on promotion (at least on booths), what their newest products look like.

You will be able to discover their major trends, what their literature and product documentation are like, and perhaps who their best sales people are. If you go to the technical sessions, you will find out about your competitors' *future* products, or at least about the technology they will embody. You may also hear something about what is happening in your field overseas. You might meet some potential offshore product sources, licensors, or distributors for your product. All this information can be yours for the price of a ticket to the annual meeting.

✠ "Experts"

Much valuable information may be gained from talking to experts in your field, such as trade magazine editors, consultants, university researchers, specialists in brokerage houses, and trade association staff members. Aside from industry gossip and rumors, they can tell you about new technology that may soon revolutionize your field, some of your potential competitors who may be in trouble, which products are good and which are bad, etc. Aside from the facts that may be learned from them, they are generally interested in getting to know *you*, as an entrepreneur who is about to enter their world. Many of them will be happy to help you in any way they can.

✠ Phantom Products

One method that is often used in order to obtain market data is the announcement of a nonexistent product (or one that has reached only the prototype stage). Then sit back and see who responds. This is sometimes done rather elaborately, with heavily airbrushed photographs of a mock-up product, or with artists' cutaways. A press release may be distributed to major journals, sometimes even using an assumed company name. When the direct mail results are analyzed and certain respondents contacted, you may find this to be a rather effective method of gathering information. Poorly handled, it may also backfire, and, of course, the ethical aspects may be considered somewhat questionable by some.

✠ Business and Credit Services

Dun and Bradstreet, NCO, the American Bankers Association, and others maintain extensive files of information on industries and companies. They can be excellent (although costly) sources of data. From them, one can gain knowledge of the size and geographical location of potential competitors and the specific classes of customers with whom they deal. Chilton Publishing Company and McGraw-Hill, for example, maintain files on several different industries. McGraw-Hill's *American Machinist* marketing service can tell you the location, type, and age of nearly every machine tool in the United States. Other business publishers also offer market data services—again at a price.

✠ PROFESSIONAL MARKET SURVEYS

The value of a report from a prestigious market research firm should not be underestimated as a tool in selling your proposal to investors. The length of such a report does not matter. The chances are slight that you will learn anything new by contracting for a market survey, if you have done the above eight tasks in this section thoroughly. However, a corroborating report from a third party might be a source of extra confidence to you, as well as to investors. You will also learn simply from the process of negotiating questions of capability, scope, and cost with the market research firm. They must convince you of their experience and ability to deal with the question that you present. Therefore, you will have to meet their "expert" in your field, and they may well show you some non-classified reports that they have done for other clients in your field, or in similar ones. It is entirely possible that they will suggest an "in-depth" study which will cost you $10,000–$20,000. What you really need from them, however, is a study costing somewhere between $1,000–$2,000, with you "helping" the researcher to understand what it is you need and want to know, and sharing your present information with him.

If done thoroughly, your market analysis will be beneficial to you in several different ways. It will provide you with quantification and documentation regarding the demand for your product. It will aid you in redefining the product (if redefinition is needed) and in modifying its specifications to fit the market more closely. You will be made more aware of what your competitors are doing and of trends in distribution and promotion. It will give you a list of your first customers, and perhaps even yield one or two "letters of intent to purchase". On the other hand, your research may show that your technology is obsolete; that you will only have $\frac{1}{10}$ of the market that you originally expected; that there is already overcapacity in the business, forcing down profit margins; that there is some built-in reason why no one would buy your product, even if it were better than that of your competitor (*e.g.*, for many years, "Buy American" had an extremely powerful influence on the use of imported parts and equipment, even though foreign-made products were often cheaper and frequently of better quality). Avoiding just one massive blunder can more than justify the cost of the research.

CONVENTIONAL ⇦ ⇨ REALITY
WISDOM

The real entrepreneur will not be able to afford the time and money for fancy "market research"—and he probably won't need it anyway.

A little effort may yield enormous returns of information and increase credibility—both scarce commodities in most new ventures.

REFERENCES

1 / Dible, Donald M., *Up Your Own Organization.* Santa Clara, Calif.: Entrepreneur Press, 1971.

This book is a regular gold mine of practical information on sources of marketing data.

2 / Erdos, P. L., *Professional Market Surveys.* New York: McGraw-Hill Co., 1970.

This is a very practical treatment of the design, execution, and interpretation of mail surveys—the principal tool available to entrepreneurs.

3 / Smith, J. M., *Interviewing in Market and Social Research.* New York: Routledge & Kegan Paul, 1972.

Useful guidance to the techniques of interviewing.

4 / Bolt, G. J., *Market and Sales Forecasting—A Total Approach.* New York: John Wiley & Sons, Inc., 1972.

A solid and very complete marketing text—oriented, however, more toward the larger firm.

5 / Copulsky, William, *Practical Sales Forecasting.* New York: American Marketing Association, 1970.

This is very practical, and useful to the large or small firm.

6 / Clewett, R. M., **"Making a Market Survey"**, in *Management Aids for Small Business, Annual No. 4.* Washington D.C.: Small Business Administration, 1958.

7 / Bernstein, Maurice S., **"Sales Forecasting for Small Business"**, in *Management Aids for Small Business, Annual No. 4.* Washington, D.C.: Small Business Administration, 1958.

8 / Gordon, W. C., Jr., **"Selecting Marketing Research Services"**, in *Management Aids for Small Manufacturers, Annual No. 9.* Washington, D.C.: Small Business Administration, 1963.

9 / Anthony, E. L., **"Appraising the Market for the Services You Offer"**, in *Small Marketers Aids, Annual No. 2.* Washington, D.C.: Small Business Adminstration, 1967.

10 / Clewett, R. M., **"Checking Your Marketing Channels"**, in *Management Aids for Small Manufacturers, Annual No. 9.* Washington, D.C.: Small Business Administration, 1963.

References 6–10 are fairly useful for the beginning market researcher, and have the great advantage of being available at the regional SBA offices. They tend, however, to be oriented toward general small business rather than the growth-oriented start-up enterprise.

5

selection

of

cohorts

I'm not too bright myself but I have a lot of very bright people working for me.

✳ ANONYMOUS ✳

Companies are groups of people. Skillful management is fundamentally the ability to attract, train, motivate, and retain good, experienced people. However, your reasons for starting a new business may or may not include an exhibition of your superb managerial skill. The main objective should be to make money. This implies the retention of a maximum amount of equity for yourself, while raising the funds necessary for each ensuing stage of your company's growth.

Backers have a powerful and statistically well-founded preference for the "founding *team*", as opposed to the individual founder. Both academic studies and venture capitalists' experiences seem to confirm that a team effort is more likely to succeed than is the individual effort. The team, theoretically, should not be one-sided in its area of expertise, but should rather be a complementary group of people whose specialized skills cover the major, functional needs of a company of your kind.

IS A TEAM REALLY NECESSARY?

The question of the desirability and size of a team deserves some scrutiny, since there is an obvious conflict between having partners and retaining the majority of the stock for yourself. Whether a team is really necessary depends upon several factors:

1 / *The character of the venture.* Do you require a top-notch performer for every role, or can satisfactory people be hired, later, for some key roles?

2 / *Your own personality, energy, and ability.* Are you the kind of person who is equally comfortable making technical, marketing, and business judgments? Or do you feel that it is essential to have a strong partner in one or more of these areas? Will you be comfortable in allowing your associates to tend the business while you're away, or is a real alter ego necessary to your peace of mind? Will you need a partner to share the day-to-day pressures and burdens, or do you function best when all decisions rest upon you?

In general, the author's prejudices favor smaller, rather than larger, teams. Despite the prevailing conventional wisdom of having teams share entrepreneurial efforts, it is the author's belief that the burden of proof is definitely on the larger team.

COMMON TEAM PROBLEMS

Teams, especially democratic ones, can create as many problems as they solve. This is especially true in cases where team members have not known one another before, or have not worked together under stress situations. On the other hand, people who *have* worked together tend either to be personal friends or to be in the same specialty. Therefore, personal or noncomplementary relationships may tend to greatly dilute the alleged benefits of a team.

There also exist a number of potential sources of team conflict that are hard, if not impossible, to evaluate before the business is launched. People vary widely in the way they handle pressure, in their willingness to work long hours, in their ability to deal with ambiguity, in their ethical standards, in their sense of humor, and in their innate intelligence. Serious mismatches in any of these areas can create conflicts of such magnitude that the presumed benefits of team effort will be negated.

Certain of these risks can be avoided by applying modern methods of psychological testing. Much is known about complementary and conflicting personalities. As a practical matter, however, it is unlikely that *your* team will consider it necessary to hire an agency for this purpose, however desirable the process may seem. Many will say, "That's just for other guys." And, of course, each person's sense of privacy may surface. Don't forget Oscar Wilde's bleak observation: "To be understood is to be found out."

THE QUESTION OF STOCK

A more important, if less subtle, consideration at the outset will be: Who should have how much stock? Or, more bluntly, why should *I* part with *any* of it? This is not a decision that should be made lightly, over a few beers with friends. It will have much to do with the future of the company. It greatly influences the direction that the company takes, how swiftly it can respond to changes in its environment, and how effectively its plans can be formulated and executed. Moreover, there is a tendency among teams to think of equal partnership as being not only the fair, but also the proper way of doing things. After all, if the company hasn't even gotten off the ground, why should anyone doubt that each partner will make an equal contribution? This kind of reasoning will lead to your having three equal partners, and leave you wondering, in the years ahead, why in the world you ever did it.

The following considerations are important to bear in mind.

1 / *Partners need not be equal partners.* **Common stock makes unequal partnership both feasible and easily quantified.**

2 / *Do not take on a partner if you can hire a person for the same role.*

3 / *Do not take on partners because you think having a "balanced team" will impress financial backers.* **Responsible backers will be much more interested in knowing that the people who are *actually* responsible for the company's progress are the ones who hold the motivating stock.**

4 / *Do not allow your normal sense of democracy to cause you to part with more stock than is needed to give your partner the motivation to use his full energies.* Try to view the situation from *his* standpoint. What is he doing now? What are his prospects? Does he have a better opportunity?

5 / *Do not allow the immediacy of your present need, whatever it might be, to bias your judgment in favor of a partner versus an employee.*

6 / *Stay flexible in terms of compensation and motivation.* Consider stock options or, preferably, bonus plans. Don't use stock when cash or IOUs will work as effectively. And don't make vague promises about stock when hiring.

7 / *Do not approach potential partners with tentative offers, in order to elicit their help in shaping your ideas, until you have gone as far as you can go without them.* Get your initial business plan in order; incorporate; get an office, stationery, and phone; and find a part-time accountant. In short, make sure that you have established the company as *yours*, so that anyone joining you will do so on *your* terms.

8 / *If your analysis shows that you can do it alone, don't be afraid of it.* If you discover, as things progress, that you really *do* need a couple of partners, it's easier to get them later than it is doing it the other way around.

If the above seems to some to be rather Machiavellian, it will seem to others to be nothing more than obvious common sense. The author believes that the team idea has been greatly overemphasized. Some very bizarre failures can be found to support this viewpoint. One or two carefully selected and functioning partners can greatly smooth the road to success, but a team for team's sake is simply a source of more problems for the enterpreneur at a time when he certainly has enough problems already. Contrary to the widely held view, the stock of a new company, rather than having zero value, is the only thing it *has* of value. Do not use it to compensate the janitor!

In presenting a business plan to potential backers, you will, of course, be expected to indicate the two or three key people who will be working with or for you. You should be able either to state who will fill the roles or to demonstrate convincingly that you understand the job requirements and possess the managerial competence to recruit and utilize people, when and if they are needed.

Ideally, the people you choose will have functioned in small-company roles before. Even an unsuccessful former entrepreneur will be a better bet than someone who has had no entrepreneurial experience whatsoever. If you need someone who has been a project manager from Colossus Aerospace Co., who has a brilliant record, but who has normally had three assistants and 100 engineers under him, consider making him a director or a consultant. The same is true for the marketing manager who functions only "first class", with huge advertising budgets, big staffs, and a nationwide direct sales force, replete with pep rallies in Bermuda. You will be better off with a bright young person who knows his way around in your industry, but whose mistakes are not going to destroy your company by sheer magnitude. If he's had some entrepreneurial experience, perhaps as a rep, so much the better. He's the person who will get out of bed in the mornings and make his four sales calls and twenty phone calls. He's the person you need.

Hire people with the qualifications you need *now*. With luck, the employee will grow with the job. If not, you can replace him at some later time. But don't make the error of hiring overqualified people, thinking that the company will fully utilize their skills when sales reach $3 million. Your job is to be sure those sales get to $3 million at all.

Offers made to prospective partners and employees before the company is on its feet have a somewhat surrealistic quality. The company has no money, no customers; in short, it is not a functioning company— yet. Realizing this, the prospective employee will expect some stock. But he will also expect market-rate compensation, even if it comes in the form of IOUs. Don't make the mistake of hiring someone who is worth $20,000 for $15,000 and some stock. Give him what he is worth, even if it is partially deferred. Make the question of stock contingent upon performance.

The proper function of founders' stock is *not* compensation for past deeds. It is, rather, to provide motivation for deeds *yet to come*. The deferral of ownership privileges for a couple of years should not be viewed by the employee as the withholding of just compensation for two years of service. The two years should properly be considered as a probationary period, during which time the company must decide whether the person is worth having around for a longer time. During that period, the employee should receive full compensation, so that if for any reason the stock fails to materialize, he will have no basis for complaint against the firm. Your attorney will be able to help you in evaluating the various combinations of present and deferred salary and stock rights that are appropriate in different stages of corporate growth.

HOUSECLEANING

In the very early stages of forming a company, you are likely to discover that you have already made some mistakes in choosing your partners or employees. It's possible that your marketing manager will disappear to Cape Cod on the weekend he was supposed to finish his marketing plan. Your chief engineer may anguish for days over details that should be resolved within a few minutes. In short, for any number of reasons you may decide you have hired the wrong person.

What do you do? He knows your plans. You've given him stock. You've told your prospective backers that he's nothing short of indispensable. He's given his employer notice, and his business cards are already printed. What can be done?

Well, maybe you should go ahead, raise the money, and keep the lid on. This problem can be dealt with later. Right? Wrong! Get rid of him now. Even though funding is in prospect, the stock has no "value", and it will take much longer than you had expected to get your money in the bank. Now is the time to level with him and make him an offer he can't refuse. Give him IOUs bearing interest for the estimated work-hours he's put in. Offer to buy back his stock at a substantially higher price than he paid for it. Offer to reimburse his placement fees if he has to get another job. Offer to retain him as a director or a consultant. Pay his price in "consulting fees" if necessary. But *get him out.*

But no matter how· friendly, forthright, and rational you try to be, however, you may expect the person to be hostile, irrational, and ungrateful. You have challenged his professional competence, trampled his self-esteem, and left him on a financial limb. If you were in that position you, too, would be upset. Expect some ugliness. Should it develop, your lawyer can suggest various alternatives. Hopefully it will not come to this, and it will be evident to both parties that the partnership just won't work. But if things do get worse, fight it out and remember that it's easier now, when the numbers are small, than it ever will be in the future. As far as your backers are concerned, they probably will not be dismayed by the disorder in your house. They halfway expected it anyway, and it will give them a good chance to size *you* up under pressure. After all, you were *supposed* to be tough.

The initial stages, before you even reach the starting gate, are a lot of fun. This is the idea stage, when the really creative architecture of your venture takes place. Seeds of eventual success or failure are planted.

The real entrepreneur, however, is not swept along by the prevailing euphoria. He has the guts to correct early mistakes, before it is too late.

CONVENTIONAL WISDOM ⟨ ➡ **REALITY**

Every venture needs a balanced team of men with complementary skills in marketing, production, engineering, and operations.	**Every venture needs a founder who understands the need for supporting skills and knows where to find them, when needed.**

REFERENCES

1 / Steiner, Ivan D., **Group Processes and Productivity.** New York: Academic Press, 1972.

Discusses current research, relating task performance to size, composition, and motivation of groups.

2 / Smith, P. B., **Group Processes.** Middlesex, England: Penguin Books, 1970.

Discusses many of the things we now know about small-group behavior. Presents research findings as well as theory.

the
fetal stage:
form
versus
substance

Analysis, criticism are of no interest to me unless they are a path to constructive, action-bent thinking. Critical type of intelligence is boring and destructive and only satisfactory to those who indulge in it. Most new projects —I can even say every one of them—can be analyzed to destruction.

✤ GEORGES DORIOT ✤

Let us define the fetal stage of the enterprise as the time that lies between the fun of conception and the agonies of birth of a corporation. This is by far the most ambiguous stage of the development of a new enterprise. Things may change radically in any direction during this period. You have your basic idea for a product, perhaps even a prototype. You have— or think you have—commitments from key people who will help you get off the ground. One or two of you are probably spending substantial time on the venture by now, even if you're still holding down a full-time job. The crude outline of a business plan exists, but you still don't know enough about the market to make any defensible sales projections or *pro forma* profitability estimates. You think you know a couple of investors who might be able to provide seed money, but you're not sure how to approach them. You're wondering whether to incorporate, how fast to move in product development, etc. In short you're asking yourself hour by hour the question, "What do I do next?"

During the fetal stage everything is fluid. Nothing has become firm yet, and this fact amplifies every form of perturbation upon the incipient corporate baby. It is at this stage, for example, that you might discover that, instead of manufacturing, it would make a lot more sense to set up a sales or leasing company. Or you might discover that your chief technical man is a phoney, and a terrible engineer, and that the prototype that he has created doesn't work. Finally, you might discover that you can't enjoy the ambiguities of the new enterprise—that the lack of a structured work day is unbearable to you—and decide to give the whole thing up.

These are all radical influences, to say the least. It seems as though a million things need to be done, and a million questions must be resolved, all at the same time. Some of these are discussed below.

WHAT FORM SHOULD THE COMPANY TAKE?

Should it be a corporation, or a single proprietorship, or a partnership, or a syndicate, or *what?* Each of these possibilities has its specific legal, tax, and debt liability consequences, which any attorney can help you understand. However, unless some special circumstances dictate otherwise, you might as well incorporate right away. It is not an expensive process, and you do not need to have your permanent attorney selected at this point. Moreover, the very act of drawing up your corporate charter may help you in solidifying your vision of what you want your company to become, and the possible ranges of its activities. Other benefits include the following:

1 / Incorporation forces you to choose a name and research it for prior claimants, thus eliminating the possible awkwardness of having to change the name six months after the inception of the company.

2 / Being incorporated gives your venture, if nothing else, the *illusion* of permanence. This is a great help in recruiting partners on *your terms*, as well as in persuading suppliers, bankers, and customers that you're serious and plan to be around for a while.

3 / In a corporation, ownership is more readily divisible than in the common forms of partnership. This makes "uneven partnerships" more easily quantifiable.

4 / It permits you to go ahead with a logo and permanent-quality stationery, and to have literature designed and produced without risking the possibility of having to do the whole job twice.

Having decided to incorporate, you may ask yourself whether you should (as many big companies have) incorporate in a place like Delaware. The answer is probably no. By the time you face the problems that incorporation in Delaware is supposed to solve, you will be able to afford to reincorporate there.

Secondly, you must decide what kind of corporation you want to have. There are some forms of incorporation in which special tax features are inherent. A "Subchapter S" incorporation will allow your financial backers to take as an *ordinary* loss any operating loss incurred by the corporation. A "Section 1244" incorporation permits them to take an ordinary loss (on their individual tax returns) from the sale of the company's stock, rather than a capital loss. Both these features operate in a similar way. They are intended to induce individuals with high incomes or large net worths to invest in risky new ventures. These privileges are, however, limited to companies that fall below specified limits of total capital, number of investors, etc. Therefore, the principal benefits are available to the smallest and/or newest ventures. Since these features of corporate law exist, there is very little reason not to take advantage of them. Your attorney, however, should examine the particulars of your situation and make a firm recommendation.

WHAT KIND OF FACILITIES?

There are several reasons that make it desirable to have different addresses for your home and your business. In addition to having a place to which deliveries can be sent, where the phone can ring, where prototypes can be developed, etc., it is a clear signal to prospective partners that this is *your* turf, and that any agreement made with them will be subject to *your* terms.

While ideas vary on the subject, you will probably be better off with an office of at least reasonable dignity. The want-ad section of the newspaper often contains information about space to share, along with secretarial help, office equipment, etc. This can be a better solution than renting an office immediately and hiring a secretary yourself. It can, however, be a bit costly. An alternative solution to this problem is to find a friend with an office or plant with the necessary overheads and ask him if you can share it—if not for free, then on a deferred-rent basis. This might give you access to other desirable facilities, such as a shop, conference room, telephone board, etc.,—maybe even a purchasing agent—which would help you materially as well as enhancing your appearance. Remember: *Appearances count,* especially at the beginning, when there is so little real substance with which to back it up. You must not, on the other hand, become one of those entrepreneurs who are so preoccupied with the form of the business that they forget all about its substance!

DIRECTORS, PRO AND CON

In some states, corporations are required by law to have a board of directors. Such a board may include you and your spouse, or any number of other people. In theory, the board sets overall corporation policy and the executives execute it. In the small business venture, however, the board usually serves a somewhat different function. Many entrepreneurs use it as a kind of totem pole, made up of a maximum number of influential and impressive figures whose function is to impress the prospective investor. This is, in all probability, the major function of outside directors during the fetal stage of a company.

On the other hand, you should not allow the recruitment of important figures to become an obsession—you have other, more important things to do. Important people tend to be busy, and are therefore reluctant to become board members—especially if they perceive their function as being mainly one of decoration. As your plans and prospects develop, it will become somewhat easier to find outside directors. Until then, however, too many outsiders may hamper your flexibility and become an encumbrance in your efforts. If you feel the need to have an "outside" officer, your attorney will probably be willing to be clerk. He has to do all the work, anyway.

It is often suggested that an outside mentor, or "godfather", can be extremely helpful in starting a new venture. This is true, especially if he is an experienced person who has had first-hand entrepreneurial experience. He can serve as a sounding board for new ideas; as a reference for banks, attorneys, etc.; and, just as important, as a source of guidance and encouragement when you feel as though everything is falling apart right in front of your eyes. If you know any such persons, get them on the board early. But note: *They don't have to be directors.*

PROTOTYPES AND PLAUSIBILITY

You don't need a book to tell you that the more fully developed your product is, the more easily you will be able to raise seed money for it and get the project off the ground. There is, of course, a succession of stages in product development that runs from idea, to design, to prototype, to preproduction prototype, to tooled production models, to sales of the actual product. You can show your product at any of these stages. It goes without saying, however, that the closer you are to the finished product, the better.

In most instances the prototype stage is the earliest point at which you should seek investors. This is the point at which the venture begins to acquire momentum. Products that cannot be explained to prospective backers in technical terms *can* be demonstrated. The functioning entity can give your designers something concrete with which to work, as they begin to actually *see* ways in which the product can be radically improved while reducing the production costs. Most of all, the prototype is the first real evidence that your company *has* a product. Your statements about its marketability and profit-making potential increases in plausibility. In short, you'll probably be better off with a lower profile while the prototype is being built, in the fetal corporate stage.

WHERE DOES SEED MONEY COME FROM?

Seed money—sometimes called *ad*venture capital—must be differentiated with clarity from *venture* capital. Seed money is the money that goes into the company before it is actually functioning as such. Its purpose is to get the company from fetal to newborn status, and as much further as possible before outside financing and its accompanying ownership dilution occurs.

Seed money is most likely to come from the entrepreneur and his partners—at least the first few thousand dollars of it. If more is needed, the search widens. Studies show that virtually all initial outside funding for new technical enterprises comes from wealthy individuals. In practically every community, there are a few wealthy people who have an interest in entrepreneurial efforts. Seek them out when your prototype and business plan are in reasonable shape. Present your story as convincingly as possible, and sign them up. If there is a scarcity of wealthy businessmen or people who are themselves ex-entrepreneurs in your area, approach doctors, dentists, and lawyers. Such professionals often have large unsheltered incomes that might make them perk up their ears at an attractive "Subchapter S" offer. Failing this, try your relatives, mortgage the house, sell the car, or do whatever else is needed in order to raise the necessary capital. Before you do that, however, stop for a moment and ask yourself whether the market is, perhaps, sending you a message.

Finally, don't accept more seed capital than you need. It is always flattering to have a high valuation placed on your company by even an unsophisticated outsider. However, the more you can achieve on a small amount of seed capital, the more impressive your results will be. It will also be healthier for your company in the long run. In the next round, money will be easier to find. Hold on to that stock!

WHAT TO DO UNTIL THE MONEY ARRIVES

Whether or not you have reached your desired minimum level of seed capital, there are certain things that must be done immediately. Some are major, some minor—but all are important.

1 / *Make sure that people are able to get in touch with you.* If there are times when the phone cannot be covered, get an answering service.

2 / *Begin market research immediately.* This is essential if your information is to be of any value in shaping the product or the company. Since such research usually takes a good deal of calendar time, the sooner you begin it, the better. Be prepared to spend some time travelling, because much of it will probably take the form of personal interviews. Questionnaire surveys can take a lot of time, too, and should probably be the first form of market research to be begun.

3 / *Have a logo and letterhead designed.* Don't have your printer do it. Get an ad agency that specializes in that kind of work. It may cost you more money, but it is an investment in image and self-esteem. Then get your letterhead and cards printed, not sacrificing quality for cost.

4 / *Get the formal business plan moving, even if there are*

large blank spaces to be filled in later. Try to get a feel for the figures, as well as for the sensitivity of your *pro forma* financial statements to variations in sales rate, price, materials costs, etc.

5 / *Write some reasonable descriptions and specification sheets, and have them set in type and neatly printed.* You cannot afford to have sloppy literature, even if it is temporary. Have all line drawings, graphs, and cutaways done professionally, if at all possible. If you can afford it, use more than two colors in your literature. If you can find a freelance professional artist to work with you, it is better than going to an ad agency. If you went to an agency, they'd probably send the job out to him anyway. Remember, your printed materials *are* your company to your prospective customers. The more you look like IBM, the better.

6 / *Give your team enough work to do.* Maintain their level of enthusiasm. Get together with them at least twice a week to check results and keep everyone up to date. Don't forget that, as president of your venture, you are a combination of press agent, errand boy, and cheer-leader—it all depends upon what needs doing when.

7 / *Don't stop meeting people.* If at all possible, keep widening your circle of contacts. Meet with bankers, investors, customers, consultants, other entrepreneurs, editors, professors, employees, and vendors. Try to have lunch with someone useful every day.

8 / *Write some articles for the trade press.* Describe your product, discuss possible applications, work jointly with a user on a story, or, perhaps, do a comparative survey of existing products in your field. You'll discover that editors are willing and eager to find a source of new and fresh material, and that the by-line will aid you in spreading your fame and that of your company. Also, reprints make impressive-looking product literature and appendices for financial presentations.

9 / *Set up a definite compensation schedule for all your employees.* Make sure that everyone's work hours are recorded and that the rate for each person's work has been agreed upon. Even if you have to issue IOUs, it is infinitely better than trying, a year from now, to dis-

tribute stock in proportion to services rendered—or, even worse, trying to distribute it in proportion to "value contributed."

10 / *Stay loose.* During the fetal stage, you should try to keep your ideas about your company and yourself as flexible as possible. You may discover a better opportunity. At the same time, you may come up against a complete roadblock that was invisible at an earlier stage. You are certain to learn things that you never knew about yourself, as well as discovering new facets of your partners' personalities. You may discover new markets, or meet people with better ideas than yours with whom you would prefer to work. The fetal stage is immensely valuable in that it allows things like this to happen without the danger of losing a lot of someone else's money or a great deal of personal credibility with the business and financial communities. Give it all you've got, but at the same time try to maintain a slightly Olympian viewpoint.

CONVENTIONAL WISDOM ⟵ ➡ REALITY

Get a million-dollar idea, find some venture capital, and go.

Venture capital companies are not interested in ideas. Get some seed money, make sure your prototype and your company are "debugged", and *then go.*

REFERENCES

1 / Richardson, C. T., "How Directors Strengthen Small Firms", in *Management Aids for Small Manufacturers, Annual No. 6.* Washington, D.C.: Small Business Administration, 1960. 46–52.

Pragmatic advice, oriented toward the small, rather than the growth, company.

2 /   Anthony, E. L., "Choosing the Legal Structure for Your Firm", in *Management Aids for Small Manufacturers, Annual No. 5.* Washington, D.C.: Small Business Administration, 1959. 9–15.

3 /   Mace, Myles L., *The Board of Directors in Small Companies.* Cambridge, Mass.: Harvard University Printing Office, 1948.

4 /   Office of the General Counsel, "Steps in Incorporating a Business", in *Management Aids for Small Manufacturers, Annual No. 8.* Washington, D.C.: Small Business Administration, 1962. 60–65.

5 /   *A Survey of Federal Government Publications of Interest to Small Business,* (3rd ed.). Washington, D.C.: Government Printing Office, 1969.

Every entrepreneur should have a copy of this, as a means of access to the incredible amount of "small business" literature offered by the government.

7

leaving the womb

Companies are like babies—fun to conceive but hell to deliver.

Gestation has run its course, and you feel that the time has come to cut the cord. You have a team, a product, a little capital (at least enough to make a start), and now you must make your first real commitment to the company's future by devoting your full energies to it. How best to proceed?

NONDISCLOSURE AGREEMENTS

First, you should read (perhaps for the first time) the nondisclosure agreement that you signed when you joined your present organization. You may not think that your product competes with those of your present company. It may be inconceivable to you that it infringes upon that company's patents, or that it makes use of its trade secrets, or that it will be sold to the same customers. But take a hard look. It is just possible that your present employer might decide not to agree with you. Consult your lawyer, just to make sure. Courts are more and more frequently finding in favor of firms holding such agreements, and the form that such agreements take is becoming more sophisticated and enforceable.

Should you decide that there is a possibility of your being challenged, take it seriously. Even if the challenge were frivolous, its mere possibility and the prospect of an impending court fight is enough to send prospective investors into permanent hibernation. Unfortunately, there is no sure way of discovering how your employer might view such a matter without (a) letting him know that you are about to quit, and (b) revealing rather fully the details of your venture. You might get some idea of his probable reaction from similar situations within the company, but this is far from being a firm guide for action.

In addition to meeting your legal obligations to your employer (avoiding prosecution), you should reflect upon your other obligations as well. These can include:

1 / Tying up the loose ends of projects on which you've been working.

2 / Spending some time helping to orient and to train your replacement.

3 / Taking whatever steps are necessary to ensure that your departure causes the minimum possible disruption in the company's business.

Remember, you're going to need all the friends you can get in your new role as entrepreneur. Your old company might be a future supplier, customer, or (God forbid) employer. In any case, it will be among the first sources to which bankers, financial backers, and prospective creditors will turn when they need to check on your personal integrity. Be sure that what they hear is good news.

NONCOMPETITION AGREEMENTS

Such agreements are most often found in conjunction with employment contracts, and if you have signed one, go at once to your lawyer and have a long talk. While some agreements have defined "competition" so broadly as to be nonenforceable, the merits of the case would determine your actual exposure. If you are, in fact, going to compete with your ex-employer, you may have little choice but to accept the calculated risk of breaking the agreement. The law allows him to prevent you from competing; however, he *cannot* prevent you from making a living within your field of expertise. If yours is a borderline case, as many are, proceed—but with caution.

WHEN TO SPLIT

From both a practical and a legal standpoint, it is time to resign when you find that you are spending significant amounts of time on the new venture. This will forestall the appearance of having worked on the project on company time, as well as the question of whether you have recruited company employees or customers while still employed at the firm. All of these are causes for possible legal action against you.

If (as is likely) your proposed business is something in which your present employer has a legitimate interest, you should consider discussing your plan with him. The benefits of such a course of action will probably outweigh the risks. If there are problems of proprietary products, patents, or trade secrets, they can be aired at the same time. Possible methods of circumventing problems can also be discussed (e.g., patent licensing, contract manufacture, or outright purchase of his design rights for cash or stock).

The very fact of your giving up the security of your job to start your own company will force your employer to change his perception of you. You are no longer a hired hand, and he must decide whether to say good-bye and good luck; whether to say goodbye, see you in court; or whether to attempt to enlist your newly revealed entrepreneurial talents to the benefit of his company. The first two cases require no further comment. The third, however, could be interesting in that you might unexpectedly find yourself confronted with yet another career choice.

If your employer likes you or your idea a lot, he can react to your proferred resignation in a number of different ways:

1 / He could offer you a large compensation increase to keep on doing what you've been doing.

2 / He could offer to create a new subsidiary company to do what your own company is planning to do, with some possibility of equity for you, as president.

3 / He could offer to take a major equity position in *your* venture, supplying capital and perhaps other resources. He could insist on a buy-out option, exclusive marketing rights, exclusive manufacturing contracts, etc.

4 / He could offer facilities, manufacturing time, marketing capability, or other resources—for a price—in return for design rights, patent rights, manufacturing contracts, etc.

Such a proposition, depending upon its form and content, may turn out to be a better opportunity than your own company would be; or, it could be that you would simply be selling out your chance to build your own company in exchange for a little security.

You must realize that your interests and those of your employer are somewhat different: You want eventual growth in your personal net worth, together with maximum flexibility to go public, merge, or sell out. Products or technology aside, he wants maximum earnings per share, plus whatever booster your glamorous little venture would give to his price–earnings ratio (assuming his stock is public). If, after reviewing all of these factors, his proposition seems to make more sense to you than your own, don't hesitate to take it. After a year or two, if the new situation proves to be less than you had expected, you may be in a stronger position than you are now to start your own company. *Caveat:* Don't discuss your plans with your employer in such a way that you seem to be *expecting* him to make a counter-proposal. This situation puts you in an extremely unfavorable light, regardless of the outcome. Announce your departure and the formation of your new venture as a concrete *fait accompli.*

RAIDING

As long as you are no longer employed by a firm, there is no legal constraint against recruiting its employees. Practically speaking, it may be very difficult to get a firm started *without* recruiting some of your former working associates. The financial community's preference for a team whose members have worked together previously is not without good reason. (Of course, you, too, will prefer to have had direct experience with the first few employees of your company, whether they are your chief scientist or your secretary.)

Since raiding, however necessary, is not likely to enhance your popularity with your old employer, weigh the benefits carefully against the possible penalties. And under no circumstances should you begin recruiting until *after* you resign.

Parting shot: *Try to make your break with your employer as clean as possible, in every sense of the word. Then you'll have no reason to regret it.*

REFERENCES

1 / Neumeyer, Frederick, and John C. Stedman, *The Employed Inventor in the United States: R & D Policies, Law, and Practice.* Cambridge, Mass.: The MIT Press, 1971.

Readable, competent, complete. This will tell you more than you want to know about your obligations to your employer.

2 / Navin, W. J., *Patents.* New York: Practicing Law Institute, 1966.

A very good text on the subject, written in lay language. An excellent background book for any engineer–entrepreneur.

PART II

FINANCING

AND

FINANCES

8

initial financing

Money is the seed of money, and the first guinea is sometimes more difficult to acquire than the second million.

✤ JEAN JACQUES ROUSSEAU ✤

LESS IS MORE

Two distinct schools of thought exist regarding initial financing. The first maintains that the more money you can get into the venture at the beginning, the better. The arguments for this point of view are not without merit, and are as follows:[1]

1 / Additional money permits you to survive unexpected setbacks, delays, and false starts in getting your product on the market.

---

[1] H. A. Cohen presents evidence that in a large sample of MIT spin-off firms, those with larger amounts of capital were statistically more successful. However, he also shows that those with large founder teams were also the most likely to raise substantial initial capital (i.e., the principal founder's equity was already spread thin at the start). It would be interesting to know how the *founder* fared financially in the companies with substantial vs. less initial capital in the sample. It is also possible, of course, that some of the less successful companies sampled did not have enough capital for the venture—an extreme also to be avoided. Cohen, H. A., *Spin-Off Organizations: A Study of Enterprises Spun-Off from the MIT Community.* S.M. Thesis. Cambridge, Mass.: Sloan School of Management, Massachusetts Institute of Technology, January 1970.

2 / Additional money allows you additional flexibility in taking advantage of new opportunities, should they arise.

3 / Visible working capital eases the problem of obtaining credit from suppliers, banks, etc.

4 / The entrepreneur feels secure, early in the game, when he sees that his net worth on paper is substantial.

The second school of thought maintains that, in the case of early financing, less is more. That is, you should raise only the amount of money that is absolutely essential for the operation of the company at each stage of growth. The following arguments support this point of view:

1 / Limited capitalization prevents major losses, and also the loss of long-term credibility with the financial community, even though it increases the risk of failure, should a significant setback occur.

2 / Close funding keeps attention and energies focused on the principal objectives and timetables of the company, rather than dissipating them by looking for better opportunities, further product refinements before introduction, etc.

3 / Tight funding allows the first-time entrepreneur to gain some experience in managing cash, operating on negative working capital, living off vendors, putting pressure on slow-paying customers—experience that will stand him in good stead in the future. Whether his company is very successful or very unsuccessful, it will be short of cash. Only stagnant or nongrowing companies have no cash shortages.

4 / Finally, and most important: If you sell more stock than you need to sell, you are selling it too cheaply. You should consider the amount of money you will be able to make by selling the stock at future, higher prices. Be sure that you *need* every dollar you raise. "Reserve for Contingency" is a prudent-sounding budget item for your business plan, but don't lose sight of what it may actually cost you—the entrepreneur—in the long run.

Selling stock in a brand new company is a little like cutting down a newly planted forest for lumber. It's worth far more left growing than it would be if it were used for wood now.

A secondary but important aspect of the issue is this: The type of person from whom one is able to raise initial capital may not be the kind of person whom you want to have heavy voting power, when and if the company gets off the ground. However, by the time financial institutions are ready to put major funding into your venture, it will cost too much to buy such a person out. Backers do not like to put money into a venture simply to buy out other stockholders. The money should be for growth.

WHAT IS THE WORTH OF VALUELESS STOCK?

Practically speaking, the questions confronting the entrepreneur when raising initial capital are: (a) How much money do we need to get by? (b) How much control do I want to part with in order to get that money?

These questions are related only remotely to asset values, net worth tests, or capitalized earnings streams. They are not at all sophisticated. Simply stated, you have no tangible assets, no net worth, no earnings. All you can present is your *pro forma* earnings projection, and investors do not credit such projections unduly. How, then, can you calculate and defend a price for your company's stock?

The answer is, of course, that you can't. Pricing a new company's stock is much like pricing any other glamour item (e.g., perfume, paintings, rare coins) where appeal is based on emotional, as well as analytical, considerations. You must try to figure out what the market will pay, independent of analyzable worth. Your considerations include:

1 / *For what price has stock in similar ventures sold recently?*

2 / *To what kinds of people do I hope to sell? What and how strong are their tax and other nonemotional incentives?*

3 / *How glamorous will the offer appear? Is it presented in such a way as to take full advantage of a hot market, new technology, and proprietary product?*

4 / *If things go as planned, what will the payoff be to initial investors? (If it really goes, they will be looking for something between 10-fold and 50-fold appreciation.)*

This issue is not worth too many sleepless nights. Your "price" will turn out to be merely the opening shot in what is ultimately a negotiation. After you have tried to actually *sell* your stock, you will have a good idea of the extent to which it is overpriced. (On the other hand, should you get your money without earnest negotiation, you will never know to what extent it was *underpriced!*)

VENTURE CAPITAL—WHAT IT IS AND ISN'T

In Chapter 6 we drew the distinction between venture and *ad*venture (or seed) capital. Venture capital, despite its connotation, is most definitely not intended for the start-up company. It is, rather, a term that is normally reserved for the first major outside financing. It is normally available only when—

1 / The company is off the ground,

2 / The team is functioning,

3 / The product is on the market with demonstrated acceptance, and

4 / The company has demonstrated its potential for orderly growth and responsible management of other people's money.

If you make the rounds with the *Venture Capital Directory* in one hand and your business plan in the other, you are wasting credibility, calendar time, and entrepreneurial energy. You should, instead, be talking to a few, carefully selected, affluent individuals. The principal share of your energy, however, should (at this stage) be put into the details of actually getting operations off the ground, many of which do not require much or any money.

WHY NOT GET A LOAN?

In order to finance a new venture while keeping all the stock possible, a loan would seem to be the most logical way of getting money. The major problem is that you probably won't be able to get one—at least from banks. Banks require assets that can be used as collateral, together with the visible means of paying off the loan at a reasonable point in the future. They also want clear evidence that you will be able to produce the cash flow required to meet interest payments. Since few fetal ventures meet any, let alone all, of these conditions, the bank loan as a means of starting up a business will almost certainly not work.

However, this does not mean that you should not talk to bankers. Your principal criterion for choosing a bank should be their relative willingness to lend you money at some early point in the growth of your company (more on this in Chapter 14). Some banks, for example, are willing to lend money to companies whose balance sheets are disastrous, on the basis of pledged accounts receivable. So, if you have made a big shipment, by all means talk with the banker about a loan.

Banks *have* been known to waive orthodox lending standards and lend substantial amounts of money to beginning ventures, on the basis of contracts (not accounts receivable) in hand, or even on the founder's signature alone. Other banks have Small Business Investment Companies through which they try to work with new ventures. It is to your advantage to associate yourself with a good bank as soon as possible. The sooner you do it, the sooner you will be able to find out how much credit is actually available to you.

Of course, there are other sources of loans besides lending institutions. Perhaps you will be able to borrow seed money from a relative or friend who does not want to become a stockholder in your company. In this case you, not the company, are borrowing the money and are fully responsible for its repayment. However, a bank will also want your personal signature on any early loans that it makes to your company. In any case, you may prefer to have your brother-in-law as a creditor, rather than as a stockholder with a voice in the running of your company.

Other sources of seed money loans may include regional development agencies, mortgage brokers (using your house equity as security), credit unions, the Small Business Administration, suppliers, and, in some cases, customers. Do not overlook the possibility of negotiation for advance payments, progress payments, or other advances that might be forthcoming from your customers. Depending on the industry, this may be the orthodox way of doing business, and they will expect such requests. Capital cost is, of course, included in the negotiated price of the products or services you are supplying, despite the fact that interest is seldom charged on such prepayments.

Your particular situation may permit you to function either partially or entirely on borrowed funds from the beginning, even though it is usually necessary to sell at least some equity in order to raise seed capital.

Naturally, the feasibility and desirability of following such a course should be carefully investigated.

OPERATING WITHOUT CAPITAL

As suggested above, there are many substitutes for permanent equity capital available to the beginning venture. All of these possibilities should be carefully considered, not only because of the effects of early dilution discussed earlier, but also because there will, sooner or later, come a cash crunch when you'll need to use them anyway. Every tightly run company reaches this point.

Earlier in this chapter, we listed some sources of cash loans. Other sources of borrowed value exist, however, to an extent that is not readily appreciated by the new entrepreneur. These sources include the following.

✠ YOUR VENDORS

A new venture's suppliers can be among its most valuable friends. If such a relationship is not excessively abused, one's suppliers can be among the most important sources of short-term capital. Most firms will offer 30 days credit to even a new company, with a penalty for running over 30 days. Other companies charge the penalty indirectly by denying an early-payment discount to 30-day accounts. Even if such an arrangement costs you money, however, at least the credit and the materials are available to you. You will discover, practically speaking, that you can *occasionally* run considerably over the 30-day limit—as long as you reach a current status again as quickly as possible.

✠ YOUR CAPITAL EQUIPMENT SUPPLIERS

Suppliers will often make very favorable terms available, even to new companies, in their desire to sell equipment. This is possible because the equipment itself secures the loan. The contract may be a lease, held by the seller or a leasing company, or a conditional sales agreement (usually cheaper) whereby the seller retains a lien or title until the last installment payment is made and received. Generally, capital equipment and plant facilities are easier to finance than are ordinary working capital requirements.

✠ LEASING COMPANIES

Such companies can, as noted previously, make it possible for you to buy capital equipment. It can, however, work the other way around if *you make capital equipment.* In such a case, your capital equipment suppliers can make it possible for your customer to buy the equipment, on a prepaid basis, before it is even built—especially if it is custom-designed, one-of-a-kind equipment.

✠ RECEIVABLES FACTORS

These institutions, instead of lending money against accounts receivable, buy the receivables outright at a discount. Thus, you are relieved of the delay and cost of collection efforts. However, factors are usually geared to specialized customers, and typically serve firms that have a seasonal or cyclical business pattern. Unless your venture falls into this category, you may find it either difficult or excessively expensive to work through factors.

✠ DEFERRAL OF PAYABLES IN GENERAL

When money is tight, most companies (including very large ones) lag behind in their payment of bills. There will be times when you must avail yourself of this source of short-term financing. Also, don't overlook the fact that certain of your employees (especially professional employees) might be willing to defer portions of their salary, or to take notes, either as a gesture of bonhomie or as a practical measure taken to avoid being laid off.

One person from whom you should *not* borrow short-term capital is Uncle Sam. Make your withholding payments on time, or you are in for a lot of trouble.

In addition to these possible funding sources, there are other ways in which you can save valuable cash while getting your no-capital venture off the ground. These include:

---

1 / *Share office and shop space (and thus overhead) with another company.*

2 / *Do any carpentry and painting which needs to be done*

yourself, in order to create offices, a lobby, etc., in low-rent space. (If Digital Equipment Corp. could do it, why can't you?)

3 / *Using other firms' capital equipment during off hours.* This could include their machine shop, printing equipment, test equipment, data processing machines, or anything else that has low incremental cost of operation.

4 / *Purchase used office and plant equipment wherever possible.* Preferably, buy it at auctions or bankruptcy sales. Such a practice can save you 50–90 percent of new equipment costs.

5 / *Use part-time specialists.* Engineers, technical writers, layout artists, technical typists, etc., can all be hired on a part-time, moonlighting basis—often at a much lower cost per hour than their own employer pays, since he covers their benefits. In some cases, you may be able to avoid withholding taxes—if the person qualifies as a "consultant". Check with your accountant on this point.

6 / *Begin your sales effort by using reps or agents, rather than hiring a full-time sales force.* Although most new companies haven't much of a choice, try to evaluate the use of reps thoroughly before hiring direct salesmen.

7 / *Have your product manufactured wholly outside your company.* This can avoid many headaches and is, in many cases, cheaper, due to the economies of scale that are inherent in most manufacturing efforts. In some areas, competition among vendors is so great that you might be able to arrange to have your vendor stock your finished goods at no carrying charge. This is, of course, a reversible decision. You can, when you wish, bring prime manufacturing efforts back in-house, while subcontracting any overflow to your (by this time well-debugged) vendor.

8 / *Try to make use of free public relations, instead of paid advertising.* Send out a news release to your trade press at least once a month. Write stories for the trade press; arrange to be interviewed about your product, company, and prospects. Hold a press conference in a decent hotel suite to launch your new product. Avoid ad agencies, and the big advertising budget that goes with them, like the plague.

9 / *Arrange to buy materials, at cost, from a larger user who commands a large amount of purchasing power.* You will both benefit, since it is possible that your volume will add to his clout with vendors.

10 / *Push your customers hard for prompt payment.* Convince them that it is better to pay you on time and let their other creditors wait. Frequent contact with the accounts payable department at your customer's office will, eventually, have its effect. Unfortunately, most entrepreneurs regard the collection of bills as at least uninteresting, if not degrading. They would much rather spend their time and energies in getting a new order or in filling one that already exists, rather than in collecting money for one that is already completed. But unless you get paid—on time—all of your other efforts will be in vain. If you can't stand this work, get someone who can. However, make sure that you, personally, keep a sharp eye on the receivables problems.

11 / *Above all, stay cool.* Don't panic, even if 10 suppliers have called in the last hour, demanding payment. If you find that it will take 90 days instead of 40 to pay them, even after all your planning, go to the head of the supplier firm and talk to him. Work out a schedule of partial payments, and then stick to it. Nothing else that you can do will go further in bolstering his confidence in you. And—when all of this gets *too* depressing—go make some sales calls.

THE MAGIC OF INITIAL SALES

On the day that you make your first sale, your baby becomes a business. Up until that point, everything is preparation and hope. Once the first sale is made, you know not only that you can get your product to market, but also that there is someone out there who will pay money for it. Symbolically, the importance of the first few initial sales cannot be overstated. It may be the ounce of proof for which outside backers are looking, the signal to backers that a modest loan may be in order, the indication to suppliers that they will probably get paid—sooner or later—and that they might even be justified in increasing your credit limits. It also does fantastic things for your morale and that of your team. You're finally *shipping products!* Put your concentrated efforts into reaching this goal as early as possible, with little or no outside financing. Such an achievement will go far toward ensuring a healthy start—and a successful first financing.

CONVENTIONAL
WISDOM ⇦ ➡ REALITY

The failure of most new companies can be attributed to inadequate initial financing.	**Many of those companies that fail are adequately, if not overly, financed. Most of these failures can be traced to inept management, of which "inadequate financing" is one symptom.**

REFERENCES

1 / Summers, George W., *Financing and Initial Operatings of New Firms.* Englewood Cliffs, N.J.: Prentice-Hall, Inc., 1962.

A *good practical guide to getting off the ground, financially and otherwise.*

2 / Baty, G. B., *Initial Financing of the New Research-Based Enterprise in New England.* Boston: Federal Reserve Bank of Boston, 1963.

Verifies the widely held suspicion that rich people provide most of the seed capital for new technology companies.

9

equity
sources:
a range
of
motivations

For the engine that drives enterprise is not Thrift, but Profit.

✽ JOHN MAYNARD KEYNES ✽

Your seed money is beginning to sprout. Most of the early problems with your product have been ironed out, and the team has survived the initial stresses inherent in any start-up venture. The first few sales have been made. People are beginning to hear about your company and your product, and to get excited about it. The time has come for you to find and use the first serious chunk of outside capital. Where do you go from here?

EQUITY MONEY

Unless your company is very unusual, this is the stage at which some equity financing is required. There are several different reasons for this.

1 / It is extremely difficult to borrow for such purposes as market development, research, and product development. These are investments, but they do not normally appear as assets on your balance sheet.

2 / Borrowing would place undesirable strain on your cash flow during this critical growth stage, due to interest payments and loan repayment.

3 / A layer of long-term equity money will give your company the financial strength required to borrow strategically.

4 / You don't want to be faced with the necessity of paying loans back just as the company begins to move. This is especially true if there is a tight money market, or if more funds are unavailable for refinancing. Such leverage multiplies the risk of failure.

SOURCES OF EQUITY CAPITAL

Your basic need at this point is for *permanent equity capital*, even though the financing may include a component of debt—possibly convertible into stock.

Venture capital sources to which you will probably turn can be grouped roughly into five significant categories:

1 / Private individuals or syndicates of individuals.

2 / Closed-end investment funds (e.g., Rockefeller Brothers, Vencap, Payson-Trask, Heizer Co.).

3 / Publicly held venture capital companies (e.g., the larger SBICs).

4 / Fiduciary funds managers (e.g., insurance, pension fund managers).

5 / Industrial corporations.

All of these are or have been significant sources of venture capital for beginning enterprises. All are similar, superficially, in that they invest reasonable amounts of equity monies in risky enterprises, hoping for substantial capital gains. However, each one has its distinct motivations for being in the business. Consequently, each has distinct attitudes and policies of operation. It is important that you, as an entrepreneur, have some appreciation of these differences, in order to ensure that the capital search is as efficient as possible and to maximize the chances that the new partnership will work out as hoped in the future.

✠ PRIVATE INDIVIDUALS OR SYNDICATES OF INDIVIDUALS

The private individual or syndicated investor will sometimes be the same individual who invests seed money in a start-up venture. He is likely to be either a self-made, entrepreneurial businessman or a member of the investment banking fraternity who may or may not have come up from industry. In either case, this individual is likely to act pretty much on his own. He is also likely to have strong confidence in his instincts and his ability to size people up. Sometimes, he will "syndicate" a large deal. Even then, however, his friends may play a secondary role, depending largely upon his judgment.

Aside from large capital gains, this individual has other motives for venture investment that differentiate him from institutional sources of capital. First, his principal business probably gives him a large taxable income. Therefore, a "Subchapter S" shelter may be a significant inducement for him (although seldom, if ever, a deciding one).

More important is the fact that the individual may simply enjoy associations with entrepreneurs and with the business growth process. He may see great social usefulness in the product being developed, or he may feel that the economy of the region will benefit from the new company. The private investor has both the funds and the autonomy to pursue his inclinations, for whatever nonfinancial reasons. He has always been, and undoubtedly will always be, a major source of venture capital.

Such a person's operating policies often include a willingness to become involved at an early stage of the growth process. Occasionally, he will desire to become involved, more or less actively, in the management of the venture.

Usually the private investor will be more willing to accept high risk, than institutions will be. Often he also has a lower economic investment size. Both of these facts make him a good partner for the beginning entrepreneur. He is sometimes willing to invest further in the company. Such investment, however, is likely to take the form of nonequity commitments (e.g., cosignature on bank loans). His waiting period may be somewhat less than that of institutions—perhaps one to three years.

It is not difficult to find prospective investors within this category. Your lawyer, banker, and other entrepreneurs are good sources of names, and you will probably be able to turn up a number of prospects through them, since your strongest prospect is the person who has already invested in similar ventures.

The "Special Situations" desk in a major brokerage firm may also provide contacts. Once you have found one person, even if he doesn't agree to provide financing, he can become a source of referrals to similar people who may be willing to help you.

Investment bankers often play a role at this stage, even though your company is not ready to go public. If they think your proposal is feasible, investment banking firms may syndicate a private placement of your stock to a small group of sophisticated investors. They get a substantial fee for this work, although they do not underwrite the offer, and proceed only on a best-efforts basis. This can be an extremely good way of raising private equity, as well as guaranteeing that there will be an interested underwriter, when the time comes to go public.

✠ CLOSED-END INVESTMENT FUNDS

Closed-end investment funds existed even before the term *venture capital* came into common usage. Firms such as Venroc (Rockefeller Brothers), Payson Trask, and American Research and Development were on the scene long before the SBICs. Some of the newer venture capital partnerships, such as Charles River Partnership and the Palmer Organization, have operating standards and policies similar to the older firms. They have had much experience in their field—albeit with mixed results. Unlike the publicly held SBIC, the private closed-end fund is normally not dependent for current investment upon its portfolio firms. Unlike the individual investor, it requires no tax shelter from its portfolio. Moreover, this kind of investment firm is reputed to be about the most patient class of investor. In this sector, willingness to invest two or three rounds of money and wait for repayment for as long as 10 years is not unheard of.

Such firms exhibit unusually high managerial standards. On the other hand, they tend not to become heavily involved with their portfolio companies' operations. The principal firms in this category are not difficult to identify. Before approaching them for capital, however, their distinct preferences as to the type of market should be considered. These preferences are catalogued in *Guide to Venture Capital Sources* by Reubel and *Venture Capital, A Guidebook for New Enterprises* by Kelly, referenced at the end of this chapter.

✠ PUBLICLY HELD VENTURE CAPITAL COMPANIES

Such companies are usually larger, publicly held SBICs, and would include such names as Naragansett Capital Corporation and La Salle Street Capital Corporation. Enabled by the Small Business Investment Act of 1958, these companies function, with loans from the U.S. government, on a leveraged capital basis. They most often invest in the form of mixed equity and convertible debt/debt-with-warrants, or on the basis of debt exclusively. Their use of debt is based on several factors—most importantly, on their need for current income to service their government loans, as well as their administrative costs. Their stock price is a strong function of current income and only a weak function of asset value, as in other public companies. Although there are about 325 SBICs in operation, it has been asserted that only about two dozen of them are active in the venture capital business; these two dozen are, for the most part, publicly held. The rest are simply in the business of making orthodox small business loans. Many are subsidiaries of banks.

One significant advantage that the publicly held venture capital companies offer to the entrepreneur is that their portfolios and investment records are public information. One can easily gain access to facts regarding specific case histories of companies in which the firms have invested, thereby simplifying analysis. The ventures in which they have done well and/or poorly are readily visible, and you can contact the entrepreneurs with whom the firm has invested in *either* category and find out how they regard the firm.

These firms differ greatly in the amount of management involvement they desire with the portfolio company. Some require management consulting revenues to meet current expenses, so it is advisable to ask (in advance) about their policies toward such involvement in general, and toward your venture in particular.

On the whole, according to Faucett [1], these firms remain invested on an average of 2.7 years. In his study of 13 publicly held SBICs, Faucett discovered that, while most of his sample firms did not, as a rule, invest heavily in the earliest stages of company growth, the early investments were more profitable, statistically, than were the later ones. This finding may foretell a shift in attitude toward early investment (or even investment at start-up stages) on the part of some SBICs. Faucett also discovered, parenthetically, that the firms in which the investments had been primarily of an equity nature fared better than did those in which it was mostly debt. One may assume that the cash outflow for debt service may have adversely affected performance of the company, in at least some cases. The areas of investment preference for these firms are also catalogued in the books by Kelly and Reubel, in the "References" at the end of this chapter.

✠ FIDUCIARY FUNDS MANAGERS

This category (although the nomenclature is not completely correct) would include insurance company investment portfolios, university endowment funds, large pension funds, and other funds held more or less in trust for other people. Venture investment never represents more than a minute sideline for the managers of such funds. The possibility of substantial capital gains, compared to other, more orthodox investments, has,

---

[1] Faucett, Russell B., "The Management of Venture Capital Investment Companies" (Thesis, Massachusetts Institute of Technology, 1971).

however, attracted a number of such institutions into the venture capital business.

These investors' policies are far from uniform, and it is dangerous to generalize about them. Some of the larger insurance companies have been involved in venture capital investments for many years, and have evolved a professional investment approach. Other institutions that have entered the field more recently may still be experimenting with variables in policy such as the size of the deal, desired markets, time horizon, and level of risk.

The portfolios and investment records of such institutions are not, for the most part, public knowledge. It is not easy, therefore, for the entrepreneur to have advance knowledge of exactly what he is dealing with. Nonetheless, fiduciary funds would appear to continue to be a significant source of risk capital, and the institutions themselves may take further steps to attract better deals for their consideration.

✠ INDUSTRIAL CORPORATIONS

There is some evidence to suggest that industrial corporations form a significant and growing segment of the venture capital scene. A number of industrial corporations flirted with the idea of venture capital in the early sixties, both as a source of new subsidiaries and as a "window" through which they could view new technologies not readily developed in their own laboratories. A number of companies later withdrew from venture capitalism, somewhat the poorer for their experience; others withdrew without having made a single investment. Still others, such as Ford and Union Carbide, have stayed in the market, presumably with good reason. And others are entering (e.g., Johnson & Johnson).

The entrepreneur should realize that the industrial corporations have objectives that differ from those of other venture capital sources. Their main interest is in building and strengthening their basic business, to the maximum degree possible. Statistical expected value of capital gains is much less important to them, as a rule, than is the idea of finding entrepreneurial, highly motivated people to work on problems that are of interest to the corporation. If such an investment can lead to a new division for the corporation, so much the better.

Certain other corporations seem to invest in the hope that the technological glamour of the new enterprise will provide a newsworthy kicker for their own stock, with the result that the firm's overall price–earnings ratio will be raised. One suspects that the results of this tactic have, at best, been temporary.

For certain types of new ventures, industrial firms may be the best financial partners to be found. Often they can offer management assistance, ready-made marketing or distribution channels, manufacturing services, and, in some cases, a large, built-in demand for your product. Often they understand the business problems that you encounter much more fully than would a straight financial investor. Hence they may be more disposed toward patience and calm. Also, they may present a ready market for any or all of the founders' stock when the entrepreneurs wish to cash out.

On the negative side, however, you must keep several factors in mind that may be more or less important, depending upon your particular case.

1 / Industrial corporations are usually not anxious to see the new venture go public. They are more disposed toward the acquisition of new divisions and/or subsidiaries.

2 / For the above reason, you may find yourself tied in, either with a buy-out formula based upon performance or, at the very least, with a right of first refusal to buy any founders' stock. In the first case you may actually end up donating your stock to the corporation if the performance test is not met, regardless of the reason.

3 / Your affiliation with one major corporation may, in effect, stop you from selling your product to its competitors. This could cut off a major portion of your potential market.

4 / If your deal is poorly structured, your business may be required to adopt certain operating policies, banks, accounting conventions, etc., of the investing corporation from which you are borrowing. You may also be required to share research results, to use the corporation's facilities (whether or not they are the lowest cost), or to meet other requirements that further reduce your autonomy. Such requirements may go against the reasons why you began a company of your own in the first place.

5 / It is harder to fool an industrial corporation than it is to fool other financing sources.

Balance the pros against the cons. If the pros win, find the biggest and best firm that might have an interest in your field, and approach it. Table 9–1 provides a quick summary of some important distinctions

TABLE 9-1

EQUITY SOURCES' MOTIVATION AND OTHER CHARACTERISTICS

	Private individual or syndicate	Closely held investment company	Publicly held venture capital companies	Fiduciary funds managers	Industrial corporations
MOTIVATION					
Nonfinancial: excitement of new venture, regional development, socially desirable product, etc.	H	H	L	L	H
Tax shelter for ordinary income	M	M	L	L	L
Long term capital gains	H	H	H	H	M
Current income from dividends, interest, management fees	L	L	H	L	L
Desire for future subsidiary, technology, new markets	L	L	L	L	H
OTHER CHARACTERISTICS					
Desired waiting period (yrs.)	1–3	3–10	1–5	2–7	2–5
Willingness to invest further	H	H	M	M	H
Minimum economic investment	$10,000	$200,000	$100,000	$200,000	$100,000
Risk acceptance	H	H	M	M	H
Management involvement	L to H	L	M	L	H
Early investment preference	H	M	L	L	H

Code: H–High degree
M–Moderate degree
L–Low degree

among the various categories of venture capitalists. Naturally, large variations exist *within* each category as well, and the table is merely indicative of tendency, in the author's view. Individual sources within the category may be radically different on one or more characteristics from the central tendency of the group.

In summary, you will never be able to find out all you need to know in advance about a particular funding source you may be approaching. But the more you know, the better your negotiating position will be (in that you will know what concessions are of most value to *them*), and the better the chances will be that, once made, the deal will be comfortable for all concerned for several years.

THE ONLY GAME IN TOWN?

There is a tendency on the part of entrepreneurs to focus more or less exclusively on the normal individual and institutional equity-financing sources, while overlooking other, less conventional ways of getting the company off the ground. This focus on the conventional channels is understandable, due to the high visibility of the venture capital firms. However, in his rush to get into their game, the entrepreneur may be overlooking some very good alternatives. A very partial list might include the following.

✠ INTERNALLY GENERATED FUNDS

The possibility exists that the company can generate enough cash and credit to supply its own needs. This is not the usual case, but it is common enough to justify some serious analysis of your venture before heading down the venture capital trail. A combination of high margins, fast collections, and intensive use of short-term capital and operating tactics *could* get you to the point where you're ready to go public, with *all* the stock in your possession.

✠ STATE AND REGIONAL DEVELOPMENT AGENCIES

The United States and Canada have numerous agencies charged with the responsibility of increasing job opportunities in particular areas. In some areas you can obtain long-term, low-cost loans for plant and equipment—forgiveable in some instances. Outright grants of money for each job created in such a way are not unusual. Attractive working capital loans can often be arranged through banks with the guarantee of the public agency. Grants for the training of new employees abound. Other schemes and inducements to entrepreneurs are offered by development agencies. If your venture has the potential of employing reasonable numbers of people, be sure to investigate these opportunities in all areas in which you would consider locating.

✠ TECHNOLOGY DEVELOPMENT AGENCIES

Also, the United States and Canada both have a variety of programs aimed at development of commercially significant technology, to bolster the economy and to create jobs, taxes, and export opportunities. In Canada, provincial government programs offer outright grants for the development of new commercial products, processes, and technologies. In the United States, the emphasis is on technology transfer—getting technology, originally developed at government cost, into commercial markets. Pilot programs have been funded in both the National Science Foundation and the Bureau of Standards for this and related purposes.

While such funds are normally not available to start-up ventures, once your enterprise is off the ground with proven capability in an appropriate area of product development, you may well qualify for such a grant.

✠ R & D CONTRACTS

The emphasis on the "Venture Capital Scenario"—garage-to-SBIC-to-Wall Street—tends to obscure the fact that a *very* large fraction of today's high-technology companies got started on the basis of a fat government research or development contract. Usually such contracts originate in the same agency that funded the founder's work while in his previous job. The benefits of building a technology company on this basis are:

1 / You are working at the frontiers of the art.

2 / You immediately have a cash flow that will permit building up the professional staff and overheads that are necessary to attract private work or to develop products.

3 / Your work will be recognized, and you will have a chance to establish your firm as a leader in its field.

4 / You may obtain access to expensive government-owned equipment and facilities that would otherwise be inaccessible.

The drawbacks include, of course, all those inherent in any single-customer firm:

1 / Slow collections (sometimes).

2 / Dependence on contract funding, vicissitudes of congressional funding, etc.

3 / Negotiated or limited profit margins.

4 / Detailed government financial reporting procedures and other red tape.

5 / Lack of pressure to develop a marketing capability.

These perils notwithstanding, government R & D contracts have launched many fine technology companies, providing the base from which commercial research and product development have grown. It is probably true that this route was easier in the past, when defense-oriented contracts were relatively easy to obtain. Nonetheless, there are still many opportunities, and there will be in the future. However, they usually are visible mainly to the entrepreneur who has already been actively engaged in the field, working with his future research sponsors.

✠ CONSULTING

Often a competent professional will decide to start a company on the basis of his or his team's ability to attract consulting contracts, with the ultimate objective of developing products as the company gathers financial momentum. This has worked well in many cases. Consulting provides the cash flow to pay the team, support facilities, and maintain technical prominence. However, this route is not without its perils. Often the necessity of getting a number of successive consulting contracts just to stay alive totally diverts the energy and resources of the firm away from product development—with the result that 10 years later the venture is still a small consulting firm hoping to get around to developing some products some day. The product, the staff, the marketing orientation simply to do not seem to develop spontaneously from a consulting environment.

An alternative approach has been adopted by some other consultant–

entrepreneurs, with mixed success. This approach envisions the consulting group as the R & D team for a succession of new companies. The reasoning is that by developing and spinning off a succession of new product-oriented companies, the consulting firm can maintain an equity position in each and still support a much better engineering capability than any of the individual spin-offs. Eventually, in theory, the consulting firm develops a portfolio of new venture stocks not unlike that of any other venture capital firm.

Here, then, is a list of five ways you can get your company rolling without selling *any* of your stock. There are others. Be sure you investigate a few of the more promising ones before committing yourself to the venture capital scenario.

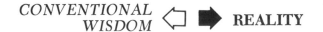

CONVENTIONAL WISDOM	REALITY
Every new firm needs equity venture capital to get it through the early growth stages.	**Most new companies need outside financing from somewhere, but not all have to sell stock in order to get it.**

REFERENCES

1 / Reubel, Stanley M., and E. G. Novotny, eds., **How To Raise and Invest Venture Capital.** New York: Presidents Publishing House, 1971.

This is about the best book in print on the venture equity markets. It is very much an insider's view of the industry, and is recommended reading to anyone seeking venture capital.

2 / Bylinsky, G., **"General Doriot's Dream Factory"**, *Fortune,* August 1967, 103–107.

A fascinating look at the career and philosophy of Georges Doriot, senior statesman of the venture capital industry.

3 / Kelly, A. J., *et al,* **Venture Capital, A Guidebook for New Enterprises.** Boston: New England Regional Commission, 1971.

This is the best free venture capital directory around. Lists firms, together with their areas of investment preference and other data.

4 /   Reubel, Stanley M., *Guide to Venture Capital Sources.* Chicago: Capital Publishing Corp., 1971.

This is a more complete and more expensive venture capital directory.

5 /   *The Art of Joining Innovative Technology, Management, and Capital.* Chestnut Hill, Mass.: Boston College Management Seminar, 1969.

This is the transcript of a number of speeches presented at a meeting in May 1969. They deal mainly with the relationship between venture capitalists and entrepreneurs and are, for the most part, very interesting.

10

public or private: what's the difference?

There are plenty of public companies that should be trying to go private.

✻ V. J. RYAN, VENTURE CAPITALIST ✻

HOT NEW ISSUES MARKETS

It is impossible to watch the equity markets over a few years without amazement at a phenomenon, the predictability of whose recurrence rivals Halley's Comet. That phenomenon is the *hot new issue market*—the recurrent wave of gullibility that prompts the public to buy the shares of start-up or even fetal companies. The hot new issue markets usually seem to accelerate in the latter phases of a sustained bull market. One was running in late 1961; it collapsed, along with everything else, in May 1962. Another was roaring in 1968–69. What happened to it in May 1970 is also history. The next one is yet to develop—but only its timing is in doubt.

Without question, there are periods during which it is possible for a totally unseasoned company to go public—to obtain public money, a broad market for its stock, and the other (presumed) benefits of public ownership. If that is so, why not sidestep the lengthy venture capital step which, after all, only leads to a public issue anyway? This is a reasonable question.

Hot new issue markets are usually characterized by at least some of the following phenomena:

1 / New "underwriting" firms spring up as though by magic. Their disappearance from the market after the inevitable bust is equally magical.

2 / Established investment banking houses also get caught up in the excitement, and begin to relax their standards for marketing companies in order to get some of the action.

3 / A form of recruiting begins, with representatives of small and not-so-small underwriting firms sitting in the lobbies of small companies, singing the siren song of registered stock, yachts, and trips to the Bahamas.

4 / "Deal packagers" roam the back streets of Palo Alto and the parking lots of Route 128, looking for disgruntled engineers, unhappy division managers, and unappreciated marketing vice presidents, to be set up in business, for the purpose of selling some stock.

The siren song of the fast buck artist is everywhere, and nothing could be more dreary and discordant than the legitimate venture capitalist's carping about sales performance, budgets, meeting profit and cash projections, and all that.

From the venture capitalists you will get a list of reasons for not going public prematurely that goes something like this:

1 / It costs too much for a tiny company to go public. Even with a Reg. A (short form) registration, the costs of legal, audit, and placement services can be upwards of 20 percent of the total issue proceeds.

2 / It diverts too much of the young company's energies to establish and maintain the status of a public company. Stockholder relations, SEC relations, and stringent reporting and disclosure requirements all divert entrepreneurial energy from the company's main business.

3 / An unseasoned company probably cannot attract a good, reputable investment banking house (whatever *that* may be). It will, instead, be taken public by Blitzkreig Securities which, as everyone knows, won't even be around two years from now, let alone able to raise additional capital for you. And, of course, Morgan, Stanley isn't going to take over any of Blitzkreig's former deals, are they?

4 / If your company doesn't perform as expected—loses too much money, fails to realize sales projections, is unable to debug the product, etc.—*then* there is no big brother to

turn to for a second, third, or nth round of venture capital. The show is, as they say, over.

5 / Everyone knows the record overall of unseasoned public offerings is pretty lousy.

Is this an impressive list of prudent arguments, or merely self-serving ad copy from the equity capital club? Nobody knows for sure, but one thing *is* sure: This elixer shouldn't be swallowed neat. It does deserve some critical scrutiny before you dismiss the possibility of taking your deal public in the next hot new issue market. Some of the counter-arguments could be posed as follows:

1 / A public issue is "too expensive," but compared to what? Even after all expenses, companies going public under these circumstances often raise more net cash for less equity than they could ever get from venture capital firms. And don't forget that even a nice dignified private placement by a "reputable" investment banking house can cost you over 15 percent of the gross proceeds, plus warrants.

2 / Unquestionably a public company has more overheads and more clients than a private one. However, the overhead costs of working with private backers are not exactly zero, either. They also will require the audits, stockholders' and directors' meetings, monthly reports, full disclosure, and general good practice that one would expect of a public company. Moreover, if Round One private money is insufficient for all but the initial-stage growth, the entrepreneur will quickly find his time being eaten up by negotiating further with the old backers, trying to enlist some new ones, and ultimately parting with perhaps more equity than he ever intended.

3 / While you *probably* cannot attract a "reputable" investment banking house to handle your deal, *maybe* you *can*. As noted earlier, a lot of the long-established houses get pretty excited when they see all that action on the street. A look at the registration statements for 1968–69 will verify this. (A review of the brokerage failures and SEC rules violations in 1970 suggests also that a redefinition of "reputable" may be in order.) Also, a self-underwritten Reg. A offering may not be out of the question.

4 / It is almost certainly true that a public company that performs miserably is more or less out of luck—unless, of course, it happens to have an investment banker with sufficient clout and guts to stand by and, if warranted, support the stock. But it is equally true that a lousy performer —even one with great prospects—arouses rather limited enthusiasm from the private equity sector. We may expect to find the backers who have already lost a bundle on the deal among the least enthusiastic. Neither private nor public money is any guarantee of continued largess for the company whose performance, whether through bad management or bad luck, is poor.

5 / It is easier to assert than it is to prove that unseasoned companies raising public money in hot markets always fare poorly. The author is unaware of any systematic study that shows that they either fare poorly or fare more poorly than their privately financed counterparts. Many companies have gone public earlier than the conventional wisdom would dictate, and have done extremely well.

None of the above can be taken as a conclusive case for or against going public immediately. It is intended merely to show that the case is far from closed, and that there is room for reasonable disagreement with the orthodox cant on the subject.

If you find yourself on the threshold of growth during a hot new issue market, you should definitely weigh the costs and benefits to the company and to yourself of going public. And if the net benefits seem to exceed those of the private route, go to it.

SIZING UP THE MARKET

Short of actually prancing into Morgan, Stanley with your prospectus smoking, you ought to get answers to the following questions:

1 / *Can you get somebody (anybody) to take you public?*

2 / *Can you get a "reputable" house to take you?*

3 / *Can you raise as much money as you need for as little equity as you're willing to part with?*

4 / *What are the costs of the issue likely to be?*

5 / *Can you get an underwriting or a "best efforts" deal?*

The best way to answer these questions is to take a look at some offerings recently undertaken (so you can see how they sold and later traded) and in registration (so you can see what investment bankers *think* they can sell in the near future). A good starting place is the *OTC Market Chronicle,* which summarizes both. You can then call or write the underwriter or the management of interesting-looking companies, requesting a copy of the final or, alternatively, the Red Herring interim prospectus. If you get prospecti from companies whose scale, markets, and prospects seem comparable to your own, you can get answers, or at least evidence, on the several above-mentioned issues. Some further conversation with the companies' presidents can give you a further feel for the markets, the alternatives that they examined, and the considerations that led to their choice of investment bankers.

If you are encouraged by what you find out and decide to take the next exploratory step, you already have your list of three or four initial contacts to make in the investment banking community. Go at them with a *brief* (two-page) mini-plan and get their reactions. You'll find out fast if your plan is a salable commodity. And if it isn't, they may make a few friendly referrals, so you can only win.

THE PUBLIC ROUTE—
SOME ADDITIONAL CONSIDERATIONS

Going public is more than merely one of five ways to raise capital for your new venture. It, more than any other financing option, sets the style for your future corporate and personal operations. It may foreclose or encumber certain options that are open to the privately held venture. These include:

1 / The possibility of selling out on more favorable terms or cashing out earlier to an industrial corporation or other buyer.

2 / The possibility of maintaining the privacy of certain types of information the disclosure of which would be otherwise required by the SEC.

3 / The possibility of learning, innovating, making some mistakes at relatively low risk in the early stages. After all, even Polaroid didn't spring on the scene with an instant camera on Day 1. *Your* big winner may be your third or fourth product.

4 / The possibility of knowing your backers personally and obtaining nonfinancial assistance from them.

5 / The possibility that you discover you aren't the hot-shot you thought you were and that you can't run, or don't enjoy running, a company. It is possible that your exit may be more graceful from a lower-profile enterprise (assuming you're concerned with grace).

The list could be extended, but the point is this: There are many considerations other than feasibility that should determine the desirability of an early public issue. We are not proposing prolonged breast-beating on this question—but merely that all of the important issues should get examined before a decision is made for wrong or insufficient reasons.

CONVENTIONAL WISDOM ⇦ ⇨ REALITY

Before going public, a firm should have a net profit after taxes of half-a-million dollars, five years of operating experience, and, above all, a "reputable" investment banker.	**Before going public, a firm should decide if this will net the necessary capital on more desirable overall terms than the private route.**

REFERENCES

1 / Hutchinson, G. S., **Why, When, and How To Go Public.** New York: Presidents Publishing House, 1970.

This is the best thing in print on the practical issues of a public offering. Must reading for entrepreneurs.

11

the
business
plan

Only one thing is certain about a new venture: it's going to turn out very different from its business plan.

✻ WILLIAM CONGOLTON, VENTURE CAPITALIST ✻

Your business plan is the essential piece of software that makes your whole machine function. It is your means of communication with the outside world to help you attract talent and money into the enterprise. It is your internal control mechanism against which actual performance is measured and to which corrections are made. It is, or ought to be, your regularly updated battle plan, providing the bridge between distant objectives and present deployment of men and material.

A VARIETY OF PURPOSES

Your business plan is a central and detailed statement of what your business is going to do. A checklist for what business plans should include is provided in Table 11-1. Although the common core of data and assumptions stays the same, there are different uses for business plans. Consequently, the form of documentation, the emphasis, the depth of background support, the statistical bounding (best/worst/expected), the line-item detail of financial projections, the sampling rate (weekly, monthly, or yearly) of projections, and other features may vary according to intended use.

The uses to which business plans are put include the following:

1 / To raise capital.

2 / To provide an internal operating plan upon which to base day-to-day operations.

3 / To provide a source of pre-established contingency plans for certain events.

4 / To create, through scheduled review and updating, a semi-formal mechanism for management planning.

5 / To communicate with directors, attorneys, bankers, and prospective employees regarding the plans and progress of the company.

THE FUND RAISING PLAN

This is usually and unfortunately, the first of the two plans put together, and it is all too often the only one. Logically, the basic work and detail for the operating plan should be done initially, and then summarized, extracted, and supplemented to create the fund-raising version.

It is all too easy to be carried away by the fund-raising plan. Documentary overkill may be responsible for as many fund-raising problems as underdocumentation. Don't forget that those who read such things are people—not information-processing machines. The purpose of the fund-raising plan is *to get them interested*—not fully informed on every last detail of your proposition. They want to see evidence that the detail, the backup, and the field work have been done—but if they *want* the detail, they'll ask you. A concise, attractive 20-page plan is about fifty times more likely to be read and comprehended than a detailed, gray 200-page job.

Remember your audience. Where possible, tailor the material to the knowledge, interests, and needs of the person whose OK is necessary for your deal to move ahead. Is he an engineer? Then summarize the market data and financial plans in graphs, and beef up technical areas. Is your target reader an SBIC officer? Then show how your cash flow allows for servicing of convertible debt and, possibly, for some management consulting services from you-know-who. Is his background security analysis? Have a CPA or, better, a security analyst, check your *pro formas* for out-of-whack ratios, etc.

Don't forget that, besides being a specialist of some sort, your reader is also a human being. Business plans by engineers often sound like first attempts at English prose. Keep it readable. Don't make it so

TABLE 11-1

WHAT TO PUT IN YOUR BUSINESS PLAN

	Fund-raising plan	Operating plan
1 / *Mini-Plan:* One-page summary of *essential* facts. Should be usable alone.	Essential. This is all that many people will read.	Not needed.
2 / *Background of Plan:* Origins of product, identification of business opportunity, reasons for market need.	Essential. 1–5 pages.	Include for future recollection.
3 / *The Team:* Description of individual qualifications. Why will it function as a *team?* Present organization chart. Identify directors.	Make it convincing. Some investors will turn here first.	Detailed job descriptions and organization chart.
4 / *Product Description:* What it is, what it does, why it's better than competitors, proprietary features. Family-of-products implications. Customer benefits.	This is where the meat is. Do a good job, illustrated if possible.	Include.
5 / *Ownership:* Before proposed financing. Description of any stock options, warrants, other commitments.	Include.	Include, with formal criteria for distributing employee stock or options.

	Fund-raising plan	Operating plan
6 / *The Market:* Present *documented* evidence of market growth, trends in price, need for your product. Include names of key customers, reps, and agents. State all assumptions.	Present graphically. Include corroborating opinions of industry leaders, prestigious consulting firms, trade associations, government agencies.	Include backup statistics and data, plus segmentation of market.
7 / *Marketing Strategy:* Detail sales channels, sales costs, sales calls/ salesmen/year. Unique promotional, delivery, other features. Line-item schedules and milestones.	Some detail and evident grasp of *costs* of marketing is essential.	Full detail, including budgets and schedules.
8 / *Operations:* How to make it, learning curves, economies of scale; key vendors, make-or-buy decision points; facilities, inventory costs.	Go lightly. Investors tend to assume you can make things.	Full detail, schedules backup detail. Projected unit costs. State assumptions.
9 / *R & D:* Objectives, costs, and schedules.	Stress the D. Investors hate paying for R.	Make sure *you* can justify. Include all detail.
10 / *Staffing:* Timetable, skills needed, availability, and cost.	Be brief. Investors are usually willing to assume people can be hired.	Reasonable detail. Try to predict what organization chart will look like in two years.

	Fund-raising plan	Operating plan
11 / *Financial Strategy:* What cash needed when, for what purposes? Sources of long- and short-term financing. Narrative rationale for each. When and why go public? Leasing plans.	Apparent understanding of cash flow *most* desirable. Also present *pro forma* statements in best/expected/worst case forms. Be honest. Have reviewed by CPA.	Full detail, including cash flow by month for six months. Graphic format desirable, as well as numerical.
12 / *Contingency Plans:* Outline general plan for dealing with two or three probable crises.	Detail not essential. Evidence of serious consideration adequate.	Include whatever detail is readily available.
13 / *Concluding Summary:* Benefits to investor. Identify major risks.	One page, but quantify if possible. How will risks be *minimized?* Why is *this* a desirable investment, relative to others?	Section on risk most essential.
APPENDICES		
A / Backup, market analysis data, independent studies, etc.	Summarize data, reproduce complete study if feasible.	Include full backup.
B / Biographies of key personnel.	Keep it short. Full résumés are a bit clumsy.	Not needed.
C / Key articles written by personnel.	Include if feasible, for benefit of outside consultants.	Not needed.
D / Table of competitors and their product specs. Estimated sales in relevant products.	Simplifies evaluation of proposal.	Include *all* detail, plus intelligence reports on plans, key personnel.

interlocking that every preceding page must have been read before the present one makes sense. Include graphs and diagrams. Avoid grandiloquent adjectives when describing your product and market.

Make it attractive. It need not be elaborate, but it must be neat. If diagrams, drawings, and artwork are needed, spend a few bucks and have them done professionally. Get the final version set in IBM Executive or other cold type. Get a first-rate printing job done on good stock, and use GBC or equivalent binding so that the thing will stay open on the reader's desk. Design a decent cover. Where product photos are indicated, use halftones instead of glossies, in case your reader wants to copy the thing on his office copier.

Before final type and printing, plan to pre-test the plan on a few knowledgeable friends. Get their comments on appearance, content, form of financials, believability, etc. They may spot some problems that you can easily correct.

Above all, try to keep ever before you the picture of your reader: a busy guy with eight other business plans on his desk, plus both phones ringing. He doesn't need vast detail. What he needs is a fast overall view of what your business is all about, and enough corroborating *outside* evidence (consultants, market data, etc.) to suggest that you know what you're talking about. Don't spell out the deal for him—just tell him how much money is needed.

Final Note: Write the plan yourself. There are consultants who will offer to write your business plan, stressing that you are an amateur while *they* are professionals. Forget it. Your plan will be better if you do it. Moreover, since you'll know all the assumptions that went into it, you won't get crossed up while discussing specific aspects of it with investors.

HOW MUCH MONEY?

It is a well-known fact that many entrepreneurs simply begin with the amount of money (large) that might possibly be available from the funding source, and then back into a business plan that seems to justify this investment. This is a highly refined art, to which this book has nothing to add.

However, if you are a member of the majority of entrepreneurs who are sincerely trying to size their deals optimally, then there will be a definite question as to how much money you should attempt to raise during this round of financing. As General Georges Doriot, founder of American Research and Development, is fond of pointing out, there are two times to raise money: The first (now) is when the beautiful dream is almost to be realized—all the elements are ready to go when the money arrives. The second is eons from now—when the product is proven and the company is healthy, growing, and outrageously profitable. Between those two points in time there will be innumerable problems, refinancings, struggles, reversals of direction, and zero-crossings in the cash balance. These will be times when getting additional money will be difficult, costly, and perhaps impossible. What General Doriot is saying indirectly, then, is get plenty of money the first trip to the well. Or at least get a substantial enough commitment, based on performance, so that you don't have to spend the next two years in constant negotiation for capital.

In the Fetal Stage, the shoestring financial philosophy is valid. Now, in Stage I, it is not. Stock sold in the fetal condition will be virtually given away; now, it has a demonstrable worth and will bring the company meaningful amounts of working capital. Adequate funding, a cash reserve of some sort, and a downstream commitment for further funds as warranted are definitely desirable now.

There are several ways to calculate the appropriate magnitude of funding for your company at this stage.

✠ FINANCIAL PROJECTIONS

Your *pro forma* profit and loss statement, based on the best possible sales forecasts, is the starting point. Developing this into a cash-flow projection will reveal the amount of cash theoretically required at each stage of the company's growth. However, a little simulation using your accounting model will show you just how treacherous such cash prediction can be. Your future cash balance is unbelievably sensitive to minor variations in assumed growth rate, seasonality, product cost, overhead costs, and collection and billing times. Trying to develop meaningful best/worst cases from this sort of simulation is mind-blowing. If you vary *all* factors against you at once, your cash requirements will appear extremely high. About the best you can do is to have an expected, a best, and a worst case sales forecast, and work out the cash consequences of each, holding other assumptions constant. However, you should privately realize how slippery these cash requirements projections really are. Don't start believing them too much. For a planning period use the length of time it will take you in the expected case to get to a condition where a public offering is clearly feasible and desirable. This could be when, for example, annual after-tax profits exceed $200,000. Do not be abashed to include a moderate allowance for contingencies. This could be 10–15 percent of the total requirement.

From this exercise you will also learn another interesting number: the absolute minimum amount on which your venture can move ahead for, say, one year.

✠ OUTSIDE OBSERVATIONS

What sorts of money has your prospective backer been putting into comparable deals, and for how much equity? What have comparable firms been able to command in the recent past from other sources? Other entrepreneurs will often be willing to discuss their experience with you.

✠ WHAT TIMING OF FUNDING IS NECESSARY?

Obviously, even if you get all your money tomorrow, it will be some time before it can all be put to use by the company. Therefore, some venture capitalists make it a point to stagger the input of funds, often based upon the attainment by management of certain milestones in operations. Your cash flow analysis will help you to develop a schedule of requirements to have in case the negotiations head in this direction. The future funding may take the form of equity, convertible debt, or even a cosigned line of bank credit. There is, incidently, a case for negotiating a higher price for stock bought by investors at a later date, since the attainment of milestones and operating experience lessens the risk that will be taken then by the investing group.

After you have analyzed the financial projections, the outside factors, and possible deal timing, then think about how hard it's going to be to raise money when and if everything goes wrong in a couple of years. Don't go after too much, but be sure that you're asking for *enough,* and that you can justify to the investors what you're asking.

THE OPERATING BUSINESS PLAN

In addition to its secondary function as the backup for your fund-raising plan, the operating plan should be the blueprint for running your business. Management consultants and business school professors emphasize the importance of a formal operating plan and, to some extent, they are right. However, the plan must be your servant, not your master. It is not something to be followed slavishly because you think someone expects you to use it. To the extent that it is useful for *your* management style, you should use it, update it, and modify it in a series of mid-course corrections. File the thing in half a dozen looseleaf binders, and keep it in a place where it's accessible to all the key people in your group, and get them accustomed to using it, too.

Try to think of the plan as a sort of hairy organic creature, not as a tidy finished document. Keep adding your quarterly sales projections to it, but don't throw out the old ones (however great the temptation). Ditto, of course, for budgets. Have a place to plot actual vs. planned results. Have a volume for market data, and keep adding to and updating industry projections and shipments. Plan every six months to spend a day or weekend with your key people updating, or at least reviewing, their sections of the plan.

Use the document when briefing directors on progress. Use it to help bring new management personnel up to speed, so they understand not only where you are but also how you got there, at what rate, and with what mistakes along the way.

Although your plan really won't be much use until you actually have your money and are able to function as planned, you should get it together right away and enlist the aid of your partners in the chore. Then, as you move ahead, the thing becomes a good place to file reports, idea summaries, acquisition possibilities, and any number of other things with major bearing on the company's direction. And eventually you may find that the plan is worth the trouble. If you don't, kill it.

CONVENTIONAL WISDOM ⬅ ➡ REALITY	
You only get one whack at the venture capitalist, so better tell the whole story the first time.	**If you hand the venture capitalist the complete unabridged edition, he won't even read the dedication.**

REFERENCES

1 / Dible, Donald, *Up Your Own Organization.* Santa Clara, Calif.: The Entrepreneur Press, 1971.

This gives several useful checklists and general ideas on creating business plans.

12

shopping
and
negotiating

Let every eye negotiate for itself and trust no agent.

✣ SHAKESPEARE ✣

The moment has come. Your business plan is shaped up, the company is now able to survive a few afternoons without you, and it's time to raise that money. You've evaluated the *pros* and *cons,* and the private venture capital route looks the least bad. How do you proceed?

SIZING UP INVESTORS

First, you should do a little investigation within the class of investors you have selected (see Chapter 9), and find answers to as many of the following questions as possible:

1 / *Who likes ventures in your general field? Who will look at anything?*

2 / *Who presently has cash and is looking for deals? Firms that have just raised a lot or realized large capital gains may be under a bit more pressure to invest than others.*

3 / *What kinds of financings are being done currently by these firms? Is there any chance that you will get what you want?*

4 / *What are the operating policies of the more promising firms? Do they want more management participation than you want to give them? Will they want heavy debt? Will they stay in long enough? Will they put in the additional cash needed between first round and public issue?*

5 / *What is their track record? Are their portfolio companies happy? Are they competent? Ethical? Reasonable?*

It is not easy to answer all these questions in advance of actually contacting the firms. However, one very good source of data on most of them is another entrepreneur who is currently making the rounds or has just finished. If you can find somebody who has recently financed his company (or failed to, for that matter), he will be your most valuable source of current data.

When you feel you know about 80 percent of all you're ever going to know, stop and make up your list of about four top prospects. This is where you'll be concentrating your energy, starting with the *least* likely candidate so that your story has been tested, modified, and refined by the time you get to the top prospect's door.

A NOTE ON FINDERS

At nearly any stage of a fund-raising effort, someone may emerge from the woodwork, representing himself as a financial consultant. He thinks your company is fantastic, he has some *unbelievable* (literally) contacts, and for a reasonable fee (say, 5 percent of the total offering proceeds), he will introduce you to some of his high-level contacts who will take it from there. This gentleman is known in the trade as a finder, or a packager. He may, indeed, have some good contacts; then again, he may merely lead you down the street to introduce you to firms you could have found in the Yellow Pages. Since most legitimate sources of venture capital will make you warrant in the contract that no finder or broker is involved, isn't it a little foolish to start out with one? He may have use later in the search, but then only if he has been checked out thoroughly, and you understand what he really is.

FOLKLORE: DON'T SHOP THE DEAL

This is the cant one hears from the financial world. Translated, it means that if they like your deal, they want to be sure they're the only ones who have heard about it, so that competition, or anything resembling it, can be avoided. However, one suspects that very few serious venture capitalists would wish to back a businessman so naive as to not get at least three bids for the largest purchase he'll make for some time: his operating capital. There are, of course, perils at both extremes. If you do a mailing of your business plan to everybody in the *Venture Capital Directory,* you will quickly find yourself the butt of some uncharitable jokes. Nobody wishes to feel he's being shown a "shopworn" deal—even if it's a good one. The logical strategy, then, *is* to shop the deal—discretely. If possible, pick firms in different towns whose officers don't eat lunch together. Try to let each firm know *they're* the one you really want to deal with. If pressed, however, be honest and acknowledge that a couple of other firms have seen your plan.

YOUR INITIAL APPROACH

Most venture capital firms consider it a bit gauche for a president to march in, unintroduced, with his business plan under his arm. Etiquette aside, there is good reason why an introduction may be helpful at this stage. If you have done your homework well, you will know that in each target firm there is one man you should reach first. He is the one who is interested in your kind of deal. He is the guy who is going to become your champion before, during, and after serious financial negotiations. You should know his name and something about him before you approach the firm.

Your next problem is to find someone who can introduce you to him, after providing the proper buildup for you. You can begin by asking your banker and lawyer if they know anyone in the firm. If not, whom can they suggest? Try some of your "expert" friends or the president of a portfolio company of the firm. All you really need is a phone call, letting them know what your deal is and that you will be contacting them in a couple of days to set up an appointment. Then it's up to you. When you phone, the target man may turn you over to somebody else, but at least he knows his company is talking to you. He may ask you to come in or to send in your business plan, or mini-plan. At this point, you're rolling.

THE PITCH

Assuming your business plan didn't end up in the garbage immediately, you'll be asked to come in and make a presentation of your deal. You'll be selling yourself as well as your enterprise at this meeting, so a little planning is in order. Remember, they will be looking beyond the numbers and the glamour, and will be much more interested in the man behind it all. They'll be evaluating your apparent ability to sell, intelligence, integrity, and capacity for thinking on your feet. They will be trying to decide whether you're going to be their next big winner, or a crook.

Avoiding overkill, the presentation can be polished to some degree. Flip charts of key financial data, sales curves, etc., can be much more effective than referring people to their individual documents or struggling at a blackboard. If you can bring along a prototype, or at least some photographs, of the product, you will add visual interest. Slides or vue-graphs can help. A little rehearsal may be in order.

Bring along your operating business plan, too, because they are going to probe your assumptions about market size and customer needs. They are going to want to know where the data came from and how the surveys were conducted. They may want backup schedules for capital equipment budgets, product cost breakdown, or other supporting information. Every question you can field on the spot without having to say, "I'll have to send you that," wins you double points. An effective presentation at this point makes your in-house champion look good, too, and will help move your deal up in the firm's work-order priorities.

RANK YOUR TARGETS

There is reasonable disagreement on how many parties one should be negotiating with at once. The author's experience suggests that three is about the optimum number. More than that, and you begin to forget what you've told to whom, or what information each is still expecting from you, or for whom that consultant who called you was working. Don't underestimate the strain of doing all this while keeping the company running and the shipments going out the door. However, *do* initiate discussions in parallel because any single discussion's coming to a conclusion—favorable or unfavorable—can take weeks or months. If it falls through, it may be pretty late to be starting at ground zero with another firm. Moreover, one firm may offer a lot better deal than another. A logical gamesman will merely rank his top prospects and start working them as promptly as conditions permit.

Some firms pride themselves on the promptness with which they can get back to a company president with a "no" or a tentative proposition. Others, however, appear to pride themselves on the opposite. They can keep you hanging forever, waiting for a "market study" to be completed or with some equally transparent excuse. What they may *really* be doing is waiting to see if the big sale you said was pending actually materializes; or waiting to see if you have any alternatives, and how desperate for cash you really are; or procrastinating and doing nothing.

If you suspect that any of these applies, you have a strong signal that it's time to redouble your efforts to find other capital sources more interested in your deal. Don't deliver any ultimatum or deadline—just put them on the back burner. You may need them yet.

WHAT IS IN A FINANCING AGREEMENT?

If you are fortunate enough to get a preliminary offer from one of your target investment firms, it will include at least some of the following elements:

1 / *A reasonable amount of equity—that is, money paid for stock.* In general, the greater the percentage of equity money, the better for the entrepreneur (although study suggests it may be more profitable for the investor, too).

2 / *A component of straight or convertible debt, ranging from zero to 100 percent of the financing.* As explained earlier, many investment firms rely upon interest to help cover their operating costs; others prefer it because, in

case of disaster, a bad debt may be written off against ordinary income, rather than becoming a capital loss. Still others seem to enjoy the illusion of control that the borrowing covenants offer. In any case, you may expect that the debt will be convertible to stock at the lender's option, or that you will be asked for options (or warrants) that will permit purchase of your stock in the future at a low price. These may be detachable from the debt instrument, depending on the form used. The debt money you raise will normally be subordinated to permit banks and trade creditors to provide additional short-term capital. There is nothing wrong with convertible-debt financing *per se,* but a higher dollar amount of it is required (relative to straight equity) to ensure that you will have resources to avoid defaulting on interest payments.

3 / *An employment contract for each key member of the team.* This will spell out maximum salary, benefits, term, and various noncompetition provisions.

4 / *Provision for life insurance on key team members, with the investor as beneficiary.*

5 / *A fractional investor ownership probably ranging between 20 and 75 percent, depending on how early and how risky the deal is.* Most investment firms don't require control, but will expect roughly proportional representation on the board.

6 / *Some sort of consulting agreement.* This is not too common, but it can become part of the initial agreement. It will oblige you to buy a certain amount of consulting time per year from the investor.

7 / *Miscellaneous other provisions.* These include right of first refusal on any sale of management stock, right of "piggy back" registration of investor shares in any future stock registration, right to veto any new financing, pre-emptive stock purchase rights to maintain their fraction of ownership, etc.

You should also not be surprised if the investor comes back with an offer from two, three, or more investors, combined in a "syndication." The purpose of this is either to spread the risk around, or to repay favors to other investment firms, or, in the case of SBICs, to permit investment beyond their statutory percentage ownership limits. One firm will generally be the lead investor, putting up most of the money and handling relations with your company. This is a fairly good arrangement from the entrepreneur's viewpoint, although it does leave him with more stockholders to satisfy in negotiating any future offering or financing.

The initial offer will normally be quite informal, probably in the form of a letter. It will form the basis for negotiation of the specific points, and you can probably improve some aspects of the deal if you are prepared to yield on others. Do not in any case regard the initial offer as the final one; both parties realize that it is merely the opening gambit in a process of negotiation. This negotiation gives the investors a further chance to size up your negotiating skills, maturity, and experience. If this experience turns them off, they can find an excuse to withdraw their offer. No deal is ever final until the check has been deposited in your bank.

Assuming that the basic agreement is at last negotiated to your satisfaction (this may take several meetings, strung over many weeks), you then have the problem of selling it to your own stockholders. If you are the only stockholder, your job is simplified. If you have a number of stockholders, including present and past employees, suppliers of seed capital, etc., you may anticipate some problems. Some are going to feel that the resulting dilution of their ownership is too great. Some will feel that the stock is being sold too cheaply. Others will resent the fact that restrictions will be placed on the transfer of their stock.

In general, you will have better luck with your stockholders at this point if you have kept them informed over the weeks of fund-raising with a series of memoranda. Let them know how tough it is to raise capital now, what hard deals are being driven, and how many firms you have approached that had no interest at all, etc. When you do come through, the deal will look a lot more attractive if they know what went into getting it. If you do have some holdouts, you should be aware that minority stockholders have well-defined rights under the law. Discuss your possible tactics with your attorney before doing anything.

THE DOCUMENT

Once all parties have agreed in principle, the investor will give you a draft of the document—a two-inch-thick monster of legal and financial detail. You will be horrified when you read it because you thought those people at the investment company were so *friendly*. Now they give you a document that apparently strips all rights from you and encumbers the company under endless borrowing covenants, operating rules, restrictions, reporting conventions, endless personal warranties, and all sorts of other unpleasantries that never came up in the meetings. This will all be dismissed as mere "required formality" by the investor, but in fact many new issues of substance are always introduced in the document. Go over it with care, since it may be necessary to initiate an entire new round of negotiation to get it acceptable to you, your investor, and your other stockholders. This can take weeks more, plus endless hours of your attorney's and accountant's expensive time, and can greatly dilute your efforts in company operation. It is this stage—where patience grows thin with seemingly endless haggling over small points, and what may seem to you as very petty sharpshooting on the part of your investor—that may totally undermine what seemed like a pleasant business association, and cloud the purpose of the financing itself. Many deals fall apart at this late stage.

THE PERILS OF BRIDGE CAPITAL

Assuming you were short of operating cash when you started the negotiation, you may be in even worse shape after weeks of searching, negotiating, travelling, haggling with stockholders, and paying those endless legal, accounting, and other bills. Your investing firm may acknowledge this and offer to lend your company some "bridge capital" to tide you over until the last details are complete and the final money comes in. Very generous, you think. However, unless you are *very* sure the deal is going through, and *completely* sure of the integrity of the investor, avoid the bridge capital if possible. Cut whatever corners are necessary to keep the company going without it (see Chapter 8). The reasons are:

  1 / You probably will have to pledge your stock as security for the loan, since everything else is already pledged. This means that *any* legal default condition, however minor (e.g., late interest payment, or inability to meet net-worth tests), and the company is theirs—for a tiny fraction of its value.

2 / If the deal falls through, the note is probably due and payable in full, with perhaps a 30-day grace period. *Then* where is the money going to come from? This puts tremendous pressure on you to concede negotiating points you shouldn't, just to keep the deal from falling apart. At that point, in fact, there ceases to be a negotiation—it is fundamentally a dictation of terms by the investor.

Perhaps if you are an exceptionally strong negotiator or are dealing with an unusually cooperative investor, such provisions will not be attached to the bridge capital note. Otherwise, look out.

THE NEGOTIATION PROCESS

Your negotiation with your prospective investors will probably leave you with a heightened sense of humility. It may be the first time that you were ever confronted with the fact that negotiating itself is both a science and an art—one at which the investor has an immeasurable advantage because he is negotiating deals constantly. You, on the other hand, may negotiate only two or three major financings in your company's existence. What can you do to protect yourself? Here are some possibilities (more on negotiating tactics and strategy in Chapter 22):

1 / *Get a lawyer who is a good negotiator.* This is hard to do without having been through a negotiation with him, but it is a key selection criterion. Have him with you, if possible, at any significant negotiating meeting. He will be able to give a dozen legal and tax reasons why some point you don't wish to concede *can't* be conceded. Conversely, he can attack the legal arguments of the other side as to why they can't do what *you* want. He will be able to help shape the deal in a tax-minimizing form, and provide the foresight and necessary safeguards against problems you could never imagine. He will give you an excuse to caucus when the going gets heavy, yet can often maintain the semblance of a friendly rapport

with the other side's attorneys. In general, the adversary process is second nature to lawyers, while it probably isn't to you.

2 / *Learn as much as possible about the man you're facing.* What is his background, education, reputation? What kinds of deals has he been signing? What are *his* real goals and needs, as opposed to the manifest one of driving the toughest possible bargain for his company?

3 / *Try to list all the issues that will surface in the negotiation.* Then decide which are negotiable and which are non-negotiable for the other side. How far are you prepared to move on your negotiable issues? Remember, a point that may be very important to the other side to win may be a concession of little significance to you— and *vice versa.* If you've thought this through in advance, the process of making these tradeoffs at the bargaining table will be much less agonizing.

4 / *Try to maintain an atmosphere of openness and bonhomie during the sessions.* Some occasional jokes and levity help to relieve the tension and make it easier for both sides to concede points that should be conceded. When the going gets really heavy and you know you're being clobbered, just call a recess for some hours or days. Tell them you have to talk *that* one over with your auditors, your directors, your stockholders, etc. If this isn't possible, at least suggest sending out for some sandwiches—anything to break the momentum of the meeting.

5 / *Remember, the objective of negotiation is not to beat the other side.* It is to strike a deal that is better for everybody than the initial conditions. Each side should concede points of lesser value to it for points of greater value. Naturally, your adversary may not take this Olympian view of matters, but you should enter the process with this attitude, nonetheless.

Sometimes, for no apparent reason, a negotiation will bog down. The investor just seems to lose interest in the deal, is always out of town, or in some other way permits the momentum to die. At this point you must ask yourself if the loss of interest is real, or merely a negotiating tactic to make you more "reasonable." If this happens well along in the process, it is clearly serious. You should take the initiative and try to find out what the trouble is. At the same time, it may be timely to introduce yourself to some additional prospective investors to help reduce the psychological pressure on yourself to close *this* deal. Since you will now have a long process of education behind you, as well as calibration on the value of your deal, the next negotiation with the new investor may go much more smoothly and swiftly than the first.

CONVENTIONAL
WISDOM ◁ ➡ **REALITY**

Don't shop the deal.   **You *have* to shop the deal.**

13

accounting-
inside
and
out

President–and–Treasurer disease is corporate cancer. The president's job is to take the assets of the corporation and drive them forward as fast as he can. And it is the treasurer's job to say, "Yes, but. . . . " These two qualities do not rest easily in the mind of one man.

* ARTHUR SNYDER, BANKER, VENTURE CAPITALIST *

It is hard for entrepreneurs to fully appreciate accounting and what it can do for them. In fact, many tend to view the accountant as a bean counter, a sort of scorekeeper sitting at the sidelines, rather than as player on the field with the first team. This is a great mistake.

Every business organization has need for orderly collection and deployment of quantitative information. This information has two broad uses: *Inside uses,* to give the manager the data he requires in order to run the company; and *Outside uses,* to permit reporting the results of the operation to the outside world, including stockholders, directors, IRS, regulatory bodies, and research organizations. These two functions, while proceeding from the same data base, are really quite different. The former looks ahead, tries to show the manager where he's going, how to control future costs, what problems to anticipate. The second is largely historical, generated by the book, for the record. While you will have some latitude for experimentation and innovation in the first area, you must conform to rather orthodox forms in the second. In both, you need competent help.

ACCOUNTING AS A LANGUAGE

Accounting is much more than a function; it is a language, a means of communication among all segments of the business community. It assumes a reference base called the "accounting model of the enterprise."

While several other models of the enterprise are, of course, possible, the accounting model is the accepted form, and is likely to be for some time. To the extent that the entrepreneur does not speak the language of accounting and does not feel intuitively comfortable with the accounting model, he is at a severe disadvantage in the business world. He must be, literally, as facile in accounting concepts as the physicist is with mathematical ideas. It is a fundamental tool of the trade.

For the entrepreneur to rely solely on common sense and hired hands to get him through is unnecessarily risky. To understand what you're asking your accountant to do, let alone evaluate his work, *you* require some basic accounting knowledge. This knowledge may come from reading (see the "References") or, better, from some formal training in accounting. Nearly every town and city has some sort of college, university extension, adult education, or commercial school where the basics of accounting are taught. The entrepreneur who has had no accounting, or who has not had it since early college, should seriously consider enrolling in such a program. You don't have to pass the CPA exam, but you *do* need the basics. In addition to basic courses, you may be able to find, as well, a somewhat more advanced offering of an appropriate character in cost accounting and control. Consider taking it, as well.

ACCOUNTING HELP—HOW MUCH AND WHAT KIND?

In the fetal stages of your venture, you probably found it necessary to obtain some part-time accounting help to set up your books, do posting, reconcile the bank statement, and, perhaps, prepare a few monthly financial reports. Now, with some capital in the venture and shipping dates approaching, the problems change in kind as well as in size. You may find that your brother-in-law's accountant working on Saturdays simply can't keep up with the volume any longer. What you need is an accountant, possibly a part-time one, but certainly one with the experience and energy to do what needs doing. There are bills to verify and to post, checks to write, invoices to be issued, collections to be pushed, suppliers to be cajoled, deposits to be made, checkbooks to be balanced, operating statements to be prepared, tax returns to be filed, and a myriad of other tasks, large and small, to be done that are custodial in nature but that must be pursued with diligence. In addition, there is a creative side to the job for which your accountant must have some time and energy. You must have his assistance in developing cash flow projections, budgets, standard costs, and cost accounting systems. These are all tasks for which textbook models are inadequate. Your systems must be designed to fit the context of your company and to accommodate the needs of the people who will use them.

You do not need Albert Einstein to do all this. What you do need is a solid accounting person who has actually set up systems in the past— not merely posted the books and turned the crank on an inherited accounting mechanism. You need somebody who is fundamentally methodical, orderly, and neat. If your workload will permit part-time personnel (say, afternoons only), you may very well fill this role with an experienced woman with school-age children or, alternatively, a retired person. In hiring, don't worry about keeping them for ten years; if they can help you get through the next two years, that's what you need now. In locating such a person, some newspaper ads or a few inquiries through your auditing firm should net you some candidates.

As the company grows, the duties of the accountant become both more numerous and more demanding. The need for cost accounting and budgets becomes more pressing, and there are additional interfaces with suppliers, bankers, and customers to be managed professionally. At this point, your accountant will probably come to you and tell you he (she) needs some more help—more billing clerks, a cost accounting clerk, another secretary, etc. This, however, is a very critical moment, and you should not act immediately on the advice of your accountant. This is very likely the juncture at which you should instead hire a controller to reorganize your accounting and control function for the next stage growth, to oversee your accounting staff, and raise the entire professional level of the activity. There will, of course, be the possibility of promoting the accountant to controller; however, this is only rarely a good idea. The person you were able to hire 18 months ago to do all the detail work would, had he the qualifications to be a controller, probably never have taken your job offer. Do not mistake ambition for talent in this area. Enlist your auditing firm in recruiting for this job; it is an extremely critical role. A good controller can make a company to the extent that probably few other employees can. For a poor one, the reverse applies with a vengeance.

AUDITORS

There is often misunderstanding as to what the auditing firm actually does. It is not the FBI. It does not come into your firm and go over every last transaction with a fine-tooth comb. Your auditor probably cannot tell you if you have a thief in the stockroom or an embezzler in the accounts receivable office. His function is to examine your accounting and control *procedures* and determine whether they are adequate and whether they are being followed. In the process of so doing, some sampling of accounts payable and receivable is necessary, as well as a detailed check on very large accounts with customers and suppliers. In addition, he will in the course of an audit require that a physical inventory be taken under his observation, during the course of which he will investigate both the condition and the value of this asset. He will want to see any contracts of a major nature, stockholder lists, certificates of indebtedness, and other documents with significant bearing on the company's worth.

Needless to say, this is a rather long and sometimes arduous process for the entrepreneur and his accountant. Normally it is done only once per year, although additional partial-year audits may be necessary in connection with financing efforts. The result of this effort is the "certified statement", in which the auditing firm certifies that they have examined the accounts and accounting methods of the firm and found them in accordance with "generally accepted accounting practice". However, you will eventually discover that these practices are far from being universal, and that there is broad latitude and flexibility in their application. Some businesses try to exploit this flexibility, with the acquiescence of their auditors, to mislead the readers of their financial statements.

✠ SIGNIFICANCE OF CERTIFIED STATEMENTS

There are, roughly speaking, three levels of "quality" in year-end statements:

1 / *Unaudited.* These statements, even though they may be prepared by your auditor, have little weight with outside persons because they are merely prepared from the books of account without benefit of auditing.

2 / *Audited, Uncertified.* These statements are the result of a partial audit, in which most but not all of the steps may have been taken. For example, it may be that the auditor was unable to witness the taking of inventory, although the other tests have been performed.

3 / *Certified.* This is the most believable because it means that all steps have been taken, and the auditing firm has stuck its neck out as far as possible.

Young firms sometimes fail to obtain certification of statements in the early years, either to save auditing fees or because they don't appreciate its significance. However, if in later years you decide to take the public financing route, you must be able to supply certified statements for the last five years to the SEC. This can be rather clumsy because it is very difficult for the auditor to certify the activities of five years ago— or even five days ago—if he happens not to have witnessed your inventory-taking. For this reason, and simply because more people will believe them, be sure *all* your year-end statements are certified.

✠ SELECTION OF AN AUDITING FIRM

This is rather easy, as there are only eight firms in the country that you should consider, provided you are a firm with national growth aspirations. These are the "Big Eight" public accounting firms: Arthur Andersen & Co.; Coopers & Lybrand, Ernst & Ernst; Arthur Young & Co.; Haskins & Sells; Peat, Marwick, Mitchell and Co.; Price Waterhouse & Co.; and Touche Ross & Co.

There are many persuasive arguments for the use of smaller, highly competent local accounting firms. Their advocates will argue that you get more personalized service; that you are more likely to get a senior man on your account; that you can later switch to a "Big Eight" firm if necessary; that the rates are lower; that you will have the same man year after year on your audit.

Countering this, however, is the central fact that out-of-town people simply will not *believe* the statements prepared by an obscure accounting firm of whose reputation they know nothing. Investment bankers in particular have what amounts to a horror of small local firms. If you enlist one of the "Big Eight" on Day One, the issue will simply never arise.

It is possible that the "Big Eight" firm will charge somewhat more than the local firm. However, it is also possible that they may have more to offer in terms of backup services over and above auditing. Most have small business sections designed to help entrepreneurs in setting up systems and in other types of business problems. All have management consulting sections, which may or may not be capable of in-depth work on some specific problem you may have. It is also true that if you object to the man assigned to your firm, the large firm will have the depth to send in someone more suitable.

The "Big Eight" are all similar in that they are large and nationally recognized. However, there are significant differences among them in terms of size, operating policies, and clout. One may be much better in your area, while another may have the stronger office in a different location. Ask your attorney, banker, and any other businessman whom they like in the area; then go call on the top two or three prospects, and see which one you prefer.

✠ THE AUDIT

The auditing firm you select is your big friend—until the day of your first audit. From that point forward they may seem to become your adversary. They will criticize your lousy cash control system. They will wish to create reserves for bad debts in excess of anything you can imagine, and also to reserve for specific accounts that may be a bit slow in collecting. They will raise Cain with your inventory, insisting that at least half of it is obsolete and should be written off at once. They will find your cost accounting inadequate to determine the actual labor and materials content of your work-in-process. They will want you to write off your capitalized development costs. They will discover that a couple of your accounts receivable claim never to have seen an invoice from your firm. In short, they will appear to be doing everything possible to reduce your bottom-line profit, for which you have labored so long and hard.

This experience, repeated annually, tends to produce a mild paranoia among company presidents. However, you should remember that they are, ultimately, only your hired hands. If you disagree with their stand on important issues, take them to task; special circumstances may justify your view in their minds. If not, you can still do as you please anyway, and let them note their objection in a footnote to the certified statement. If difficulties persist, you may be justified in changing auditors. The great umbrella of "generally accepted accounting practice" may, in the hands of a different firm, cover you, too.

BUDGETS AND CONTROL

The budget is a rather key tool in your effort to operate your company. It is, in essence, the connecting linkage between your business plan and your organization—the piston rod connecting your power source with your drive wheels. Formal budgets serve a lot of useful purposes, and only a very foolish president would try to function for long without them. The budget is:

1 / *A tool for implementing plans.* In this role, the budget states, in detail, how much money and calendar time are to be allocated for each purpose in the pursuit of the business plan. It states who will spend the monies, what his authorization will be, and for what materials and services it will be spent. To this extent, the company's budgets are more or less an elaboration of the financial projections of the business plan.

2 / *A tool for communication.* The budget and the process that produces it provide one of the principal means of communicating the exact plan of operation throughout the organization. As finally published, the budget will tell everyone precisely what his spending limits will be for accomplishing each task. It is your *only quantitative statement* of corporate priorities. To the extent that your managers submit budgetary proposals for consideration, they are communicating in a most quantitative form their plans and priorities for carrying out their functions.

3 / *A tool for cost control.* By considering in advance the necessary amounts for each class of expenditure, and by getting each manager committed to that statement of expenditures, you have the rudiments for achieving financial control. By reporting actual expenditures against budget, you have a monthly historical record of (a) how good your budget was, and (b) how good a job your people have done in controlling costs. To provide tighter control as indicated, and to permit the *prevention* (as opposed to reporting) of over-budget expenditures, you may wish to have your accountant maintain *daily* tallies of expenditure requests, purchase orders cut, etc., and notify the appropriate parties when the budget for a particular item is *about* to be exceeded. It is only at this level that you actually have control of costs. The monthly budgets versus the actual profit and loss statement will only highlight major areas of overrun or underrun for future management action, but the money is already gone. *Caution:* Budgets can also hide a good deal of information. For example, a department that is consistently within its overall budget may be using savings in one area to hide gross inefficiency or other problems in another. Be sure your budget has enough detail to pinpoint the reality of the situation.

4 / *A tool for assessment of employee performance.* Sad to say, the ability to meet goals on budget is among the few quantitative measures of employee performance available to presidents. For this reason it is probably overstressed, but unsatisfactory performance in the spending area usually connotes problems. Each manager must assume responsibility for the controllable (i.e., nonoverhead or distributed) costs of his area of the business. To the extent that he helps to set his own goals and budgets, he must be responsible for meeting them—not merely for a mounting forensic attack on the "unrealistic" budget. Unless every manager accepts this fundamental responsibility, your business plan, your cash projections, and your intended profits will all be blown to hell.

For all of these reasons, it is imperative that even start-up ventures establish some form of formal budgeting as early as feasible. When resources are limited, there will be hard tradeoffs to be made, and everyone on the team should have a voice in how these are made and implemented. Probably once per quarter is adequate for a full budget update. Procedurally, one starts with an updated sales forecast and works down through the P&L line items, entering costs as they *will be* (as opposed to *have been*) during the next four quarters. Avoid the temptation to merely insert last quarter's estimates; challenge each line item, and be sure that it deserves all that is being spent on it. Where could cuts be made if necessary? Improvements postponed? Capital equipment deferred? For which jobs are we over-specifying skills? These are the sorts of questions that should be asked, every quarter at least, of each operating manager.

Your first few budgets will probably be terrible; they will evoke a hue and cry from their victims, and the results may be rather discouraging to you. Don't quit trying, however; keep refining, improving categories, pushing for compliance, and creating an attitude of recognition for the people who achieve their targets. This is the only way that your costs will come under your control and stay there.

Final Note: Don't overdo it. Too much detail, too much frequency can drown a budget system in its own paperwork. Be sure the system is your servant—not your master.

REFERENCES

1 / Heckert, J. B., and J. D. Willson, *Business Budgeting and Control* (3rd ed.). New York: Roland Press, 1967.

This is an excellent work, showing in some detail how to develop business plans into budgets, then controlling the firm through the budgets. Takes up where accounting texts leave off.

2 / Myer, John N., *Accounting for Non-Accountants* (1st ed.). New York: New York University Press, 1947.

This is oriented toward understanding, rather than how-to-do-it detail. A good substitute for a course in beginning accounting.

3 / Lasser, J. K., *Handbook of Accounting Methods* (3rd ed.). New York: D. Van Nostrand Co. Inc., 1964.

This book gives suggested forms and methods on an industry-by-industry basis. Also has good sections on electronic data processing in accounting, stock registration, and other practical issues. A fine reference book.

4 / Overmyer, W. S., "**Picking an Auditor for Your Firm**", in *Small Marketers Aids, Annual No. 4*. Washington D.C.: Small Business Administration, 1962.

Practical advice for the small businessman, rather than the growth-oriented president. Not bad, though.

5 / Witschey, R. E., "**Public Accounting Services for Small Manufacturers**", in *Small Business Management Series, No. 5*. Washington, D.C.: Small Business Administration, 1954.

14

care
and
feeding
of
bankers

*A banker is a fellow who offers to lend you his umbrella
when it isn't raining.*

* ANONYMOUS *

It is common currency among entrepreneurs that bankers are parsi-
monious, hidebound, unimaginative, and timid to the point of irra-
tionality. However, it is time the truth was bared: *Some are not.* It is
incumbent on the entrepreneur bent on survival to find a bank in that
small category and cultivate a relationship as one would cultivate a
garden of beautiful flowers.

DIFFERENCES AMONG BANKS

To the outsider looking in, most banks look alike. They all offer about
the same services, pay about the same interest on deposits, charge about
the same on comparable loans. However, there are differences among
banks. Some of the more obvious gross differences are in asset size (general clout), net worth (stability), region served, number of specialized
departments, general prestige. However, most of these don't make too
much difference to the entrepreneur. The differences that *do* matter
include:

1 / *Source of income.* If you are dealing with a bank that
depends mainly on mortgages for income, your loan requirements aren't going to get much priority.

2 / *Capacity for working with small firms.* Banks vary radically in this regard. Some regard a start up company

as just one more bad risk; others see it as an opportunity. Some have departments or SBIC connections for dealing with the smaller enterprise. Have they made unsecured loans to small firms lately?

3 / ***Reputation for staying in when the going gets rough.*** Did they call in their small business demand notes (or fail to renew) in 1970, when even their old, established customers were crying for cash, or did they hang in there? You can get some interesting insight into bank behavior by talking to entrepreneurs who have been in business since, say, 1968.

4 / ***General creativity of approach.*** Do they just look at your balance sheet and faint, or do they try to suggest constructive financial alternatives (e.g., rotating receivables financing, factoring, leasing, negotiating contract advances, etc.)? Some banks are more adept at this than others. Also, within a given bank, individual officers tend to vary widely in level of creativity. As a New England bank is fond of saying, "The man you talk to *is* the bank."

SELECTING A BANK

Bank selection, though not so irreversible as many other business decisions, is a very important step for the entrepreneur. You begin investing in a good relationship, starting Day One. If your choice is a poor one and you have to switch after two years, that's two years of effort and investment in credibility down the drain. Select the right bank early, and begin grooming it against the day you really need it; when your cash crunch finally comes, it will be too late to start shopping.

Following are some guidelines for bank selection:

1 / **Develop a list of criteria; then refine them into questions you will put to the various bank officers you interview.**

2 / **Ask other entrepreneurs to describe their experiences with their banks. After you've talked with a few people, a general pattern may begin to emerge. Be sure to find out who their lending officer is at each candidate bank.**

3 / Ask your accounting firm, your lawyer, and your god-father for suggestions on banking connections.

4 / Talk to a few different banks, even if you're convinced you know where you ought to be banking. Try to calibrate the differences for yourself.

5 / In interviewing the officer, be sure to ask for some small-business customer references.

In the selection process, keep in mind that institutions are only agglomerations of people and that as their personnel makeup changes, so do their policies and attitudes. For example, a bank with a long record of working with smaller firms may have lost one or two spark-plug officers who emphasized and championed that part of the business—and, therefore, no longer be too strong or interested in more new-venture business. Or they may just have attracted so much of it that they are not seeking more. Or money may be so tight at the moment that they are not seeking any but the very highest quality lending opportunities. Thus, what you must search out is a bank and officer that you can work with *now* and *over the next several years*. What it did in the past is important, but not of itself decisive.

GROOMING THE RELATIONSHIP

To the extent that your side of the banking relationship is active rather than passive, you will be maximizing your chances of long-term cooperation. Some of the steps you can take without investing much energy include the following:

1 / *Keep your banker informed.* This applies *whether or not* you have a loan outstanding. Place him on your public relations mailing list, your key customer news-letter list, etc. Be sure he gets a set of operating statements monthly, and the audited annual statements while they're still fresh.

2 / *See him in person.* Bankers are big believers in press-

ing the flesh. Once a month is probably too often, but once per quarter might be about right. Have him to your office and review the operating results and the projections. Have a look at the plant and review R & D in progress. Fill him in on key customers and prospects, and get his subconscious working on possible other business sources for you. Have lunch, and establish some human contact. Get him *interested* in what the company and you are doing. Remember, if you do a good job now, you'll want to take your banker with you in your *next* company. Likewise, if he changes banks, it may be beneficial to move your account with him. Banking is at the root a business of people, of mutual confidence and assumed integrity.

3 / *Start borrowing.* Even if the company has $500,000 cash from fund-raising, now is the time to begin establishing a record for businesslike borrowing and on-time repayment. It is also time to let the bank start making a few dollars on your account, which they will be only too happy to do—if you have a bundle of cash. If you don't, then you probably need a bank loan, and it's high time to start learning to use bank credit constructively.

4 / *Meet your targets.* Everything that can be said about the importance of meeting targets applies in spades to the banking relationship. If you acquire a reputation for sloppy cash management, poor planning, or feeble follow-through on your plans, your bank will be lukewarm on your account—*even if you're growing and profitable.* A few minor targets met *on-time, on-budget* early in the game will let the banker stop worrying so much about you. Be sure he (and everyone else) knows about it when targets are hit.

MISCELLANEOUS SERVICES OF BANKS

There are a number of formal and informal services that your bank can render once you're rolling together. These can be worth a lot of money and should be used:

1 / *Credit checks.* You probably won't be able to justify

the annual fees for credit agencies such as Dun & Bradstreet at first, and maybe you'll never need to. Your bank has access to all of them. This can also be a useful route for sizing up prospective customers and competition.

2 / *Equity financing.* Banks with SBICs can work directly with you; others can often put you in touch with investors or investment bankers who would not otherwise be accessible to you.

3 / *Product leasing.* If you sell capital equipment, the bank may be willing to help you develop a leasing plan to offer to your customers.

4 / *Equipment financing.* When you need capital equipment, your banker may be able to show you how to "afford" it earlier than you thought.

5 / *Export-related services.* Banks with strong foreign contacts can advise you on letters of credit, export credit insurance, foreign bank drafts, and other arcana of international finance.

6 / *Payroll and other accounting.* Banks increasingly offer data processing services to their customers; their rates are of necessity competitive with outside data processing services.

7 / *Tax advice and services.* Certain banks are set up to do a substantial amount of tax-related work for company clients.

8 / *General business advice.* Your officer may prove to be a valuable sounding board and source of advice on business problems. You may get suggestions as to possible sources of business, ways to deal with particular delinquent accounts, methods for setting up payroll and other labor-intensive accounts. Besides sources for additional capital, he may know firms that might be interested in acquiring or being acquired.

DAY-TO-DAY BANKING

It may be desirable to maintain a small account with a local bank with offices very nearby. This will not be for the purpose of borrowing (although don't rule them out) but for the convenience of your employees. They need a place to cash their paychecks and do personal banking. Your accountant will occasionally need a certified or cashier's check on short notice, and a safe deposit box for certain documents. Your petty cash box will need refreshing periodically. These are all functions for which you want a nearby bank. In addition to this bank, you may wish at some point to establish a discreet account with a *third* bank, in which to keep a portion of the company assets to protect them against being frozen by a creditors' committee or a court action. Such an action, brought to make you do something you don't want to do, can be extremely awkward if you have not anticipated it.

Parting Shot: Remember, your banker is the fellow who's going to rent you working capital that you'd otherwise have to buy with undervalued stock. He's going to do a lot, therefore, toward making you rich. Treat your relationship accordingly.

REFERENCES

1 / Reiter, E. F., "How To Choose Your Banker Wisely", in *Management Aids for Small Business, Annual No. 2.* Washington, D.C.: Small Business Administration, 1958. 69–75.

Practical ideas, but relating more to the small businessman than to the president of a high-growth firm.

15

the
next
round
of
financing

Take the money and run.

✳ WOODY ALLEN ✳

FINANCING FUTURE GROWTH

Raising money for a small, growing firm is seldom easy. However, difficulty comes in all sizes, and, in the present context, raising money to *continue the growth of sales and profits* is a snap, compared to raising money to finance past losses.

The company that has met its targets, that has the firm support of its stockholders, bankers, and employees, has a variety of choices it can make. It may seek additional capital from its old stockholders, it may seek out funding from venture capital firms, it may arrange a private placement of stock through an investment banker, or it may elect to go public. Possibly it will be attractive enough at this point to elicit acquistion interest from another company. Its optimum strategy at this time is to maximize the net worth of the existing stockholders, given the total scenario of events that each choice implies.

The course of action with the highest present value (future revenues discounted back to the present) would, normally, be the one selected. This may or may not be the same course of action that yields the highest *immediate* return. For example, you may receive an offer to buy the entire company for $1 million ($1.00/share, assuming one million shares exist). The founders and the original investors walk away with a pocket full of cash and a handsome capital gain. You may also have the alternative, however, of selling one-third of the company for $250,000 in working capital. Not too attractive, you say. Not only is

165

the value per share lower, but also neither you nor the other stockholders get any cash. Plus the old investors grumble that they paid as much but took all the risk. However, based on present growth, you think that the $250,000 would carry the firm another 10 months, by which time a public offering could be arranged. In such an offering, the company could raise perhaps $1 million for 20 percent of the stock; thereafter, a secondary issue could perhaps be arranged to generate some working capital and stockholder liquidity, perhaps in 12 more months. Let us then compare two possible cases, with some illustrative numbers.

CASE 1: SELL OUT FOR $1 MILLION

	Number of shares owned	Cost basis	Sale price	Net gain
Founders @ $.01	750,000	$7,500	$750,000	$742,500
Original investors @ $.50	250,000	$125,000	$250,000	$125,000

In this case, the founders will probably be required to stay and operate the company for two to five years, depending on the buyer.

CASE 2: SELL ONE-THIRD OF COMPANY FOR $250,000; THEN GO PUBLIC FOR $1 MILLION = 20 PERCENT

	Number of shares owned	Cost basis	Sale price	Net gain
Founders @ $.01	750,000	$7,500	$3,000,000 *	$2,992,500
Original investors @ $.50	250,000	$125,000	$1,000,000	$875,000
New investors @ $.50	500,000	$250,000	$2,000,000	$1,750,000
Public @ $2.67	375,000	$1,000,000	$1,500,000	$500,000

* Assumes that a secondary offering at $4.00 is possible. However, this value will be only paper worth for a substantial period of time for the founders.

It is to be acknowledged that the foregoing example contains some heroic assumptions: to wit, that the management and original stockholders had perfect knowledge of some unknowables:

1 / The price and time when the company could go public.

2 / The price and time when a secondary offering and registration of letter stock would be feasible.

3 / The ability of the management and initial investors to sell all their stock in the secondary offering. However, this is not necessary if we simply take the market price of $4.00 as a reasonable basis for computing "gain."

The principal point is that decisions based on the relative "dilution" of capital value, loss of "control," or immediacy of cashout can be very poor decisions. The public issue remains the major avenue for realization of the full rewards of entrepreneurship. If you relinquish the possibility too early or too cheaply, you will have lost the ball game in the final inning. In the illustration, our founders quadrupled their gains over the sellout case; moreover, had they sold out they would have relinquished their opportunity to go entrepreneuring again for the next several years, due to their employment agreements. Thus, the opportunity cost of the sellout is probably even in excess of the loss in sale price. A little simulation along these lines, looking at various assumptions about the future, can help a great deal in clearing up your own thinking.

An on-target company seeking Round Two capital has a rather broader range of choices available than it had for Round One. Many venture capital and other institutions invest *only* in Round Two situations; most venture capitalists are more comfortable with this situation. You may also be able to entice in funds from insurance companies, college endowments, or other quasi-fiduciary institutions, once you have a winning track record.

WHO NEEDS THOSE GUYS?

A peculiar phenomenon occurs in Round Two financing with sufficient frequency to warrant some comment. It is the "who-needs-those-guys" effect—"those guys" being the old investors. It often happens that, after struggling with the entrepreneur through the pains and risks of start up and the agonizing initial couple of years of operations, the original investors cannot or will not put up the Round Two money. They may be fully invested by then in other ventures; they may have specific preference for start up or Round One investments; or they may simply have reached what they consider a prudent limit for investment in one deal.

At this stage then, the entrepreneur starts looking for new sources of money. Enter Mr. Round Two Deal Man. He looks at the company and likes it—*except* for one thing: Those old stockholders hold "too much" of the company. *"Who needs those guys?"* he asks you. "After all, *they* aren't going to contribute any further to the company's progress. *They* will simply be sitting on a pile of cheap stock that rightfully ought to be in the hands of management and new investors. *They* are just going to be a pain in the neck, a source of trouble, and a possible veto on later financial dealings. Let's get them out."

Herein lie the seeds of a great error. When Mr. Round Two says, "Let's you and them fight," he is getting forces in motion that could tear your fragile new company apart, literally. If he makes an offer contingent on forcing out the old stockholders (e.g., by offering them an unreasonably low price and insisting everyone sell), he will be pitting you against them with nothing to lose himself. If the deal falls through, he walks away to another one. Meanwhile, he has convinced you that the old backers are a bunch of mendacious parasites, while they are now convinced that you are a thief and a bounder, trying to deny them a reasonable reward for taking the front-end risk and hanging on with you. The damage that is thereby inflicted on the company may be irreparable. You will no longer be partners and the emphasis will shift from a joint seeking of corporate goals to one of maneuvering, one-upsmanship, and defense of personal interest. It is now impossible, because of the suspicions created, to approach *any* new investor with a united front, and no investor wants to buy into a fratricidal family struggle. Moreover, your manifest willingness to dump your old investors over the side will permit the prospective Mr. Round Two to vividly project himself into their position two years hence.

This is not to say that there is never cause to take out some old investors in seeking new capital. Some may want out; others may be willing to get out if they feel that it is in the company's best interest. However, if they feel you attempted to cheat them or to force them out on unfair terms, they will always resent it, and it will come back to haunt you. You personally have nothing to lose by pressing Mr. Round Two for a fairer deal for your old investors. He may not agree, but he should at least respect your commitment to treating investors fairly.

FINANCING PAST LOSSES

Any reasonably intelligent entrepreneur can probably find ample capital for Rounds Two and Three and Four—if his company is growing, profitable, and reasonably near target. The real test of entrepreneurial skill, however, comes when you are in some combination of the following circumstances:

1 / You are out of cash.

2 / You are losing money.

3 / You are far behind sales targets and other company goals.

4 / Capital intended for market development and production facilities has been eaten up by development delays and operating losses.

If this is your situation, you have your work cut out for you.

The first thing to do is to take a hard look at the next few months' cash flow and determine whether you can keep the doors open; there is nothing so certain to sabotage any negotiation for capital as the joint recognition that the company is in utterly desperate straits. It is, in fact, no longer a negotiation, but a unilateral dictation of terms.

If you see that the company is headed full speed for a cash cliff, take immediate steps to alleviate it. Drastic measures may be warranted, even though they may be somewhat embarrassing to your "growth company" image. It is vitally important to get the cash flow positive and to be negotiating from a viable position. It will also vastly enhance your position to be able to show that the company is currently in the black (temporarily) in addition to having positive cash.

The measures you will take will be the obvious ones: Cut personnel expenses by discharging some people, furloughing the more valuable people, and asking the key people to accept some deferral and temporary cut in salary. Try a four-day week (32 hours) in the shop for a while; if people sense that it is only temporary you may not lose anybody.

Cut all other discretionary expenses, and consider various forms of postponement buying (e.g., on operating supplies, expendable tools, materials). Stretch out your vendors, and arrange financing on any unpledged assets. Try selling off underutilized equipment and inventory. Try subleasing some plant space. In addition, you must consider lending the company some money yourself, and obtaining short-term loans from whatever quarter possible.

When your business plan has been fully updated for selling purposes, you should take to the road. In addition, try putting your stockholders to work exercising their contacts and making pitches to possible investors.

Your selling posture is in essence:

1 / The company is about to take off and realize its multimillion-dollar potential.

2 / The heavy risks and expenses are all behind now, and the bill was footed by someone else.

3 / The commitment and determination of the management team have been amply demonstrated by the tough times you've ground through.

4 / The adverse market conditions (if any) have been as tough on the competition as on you. In fact, they may be about to throw in the towel.

5 / The prolonged development cycle, with its attendant expense, has resulted in a far better product than originally conceived.

6 / There's still time for an astute investor to get in on the ground floor (indeed—you haven't even left it yet).

ACQUIRING AN ACQUIRER

You may discover after some exposure to the investment community that the money you need at this stage simply is not available on any kind of reasonable terms. If so, it may be time to start looking for a company with some logical reason for wanting to acquire you. There are, of course, many noninvestment reasons why a going concern would be interested in buying you, despite your past record and current distress.

1 / Quick entry into a new market (yours).

2 / Expansion of their present market by annexing your customers.

3 / A cheaper, faster way into a new technology or product than designing it.

4 / A source of supply for some needed products or capability (vertical integration).

5 / A captive customer for some of *their* products.

6 / A means of absorbing existing overheads (factory space, machine time, sales force, dealer base).

7 / A PR tool for asserting their support of minority enterprise (if applicable).

8 / A source of some pizzaz to get their stock moving.

Armed with this list of possible motives, start your search for possible corporate partners, first on a local basis—then in a widening circle. This may not be the point at which you would normally have wanted to be bought out—but acquisition may be the right answer. The acquiring company may be able to add a lot of things besides money to make your venture go, and the personal risks to you may be diminished a full order of magnitude.

Other routes may be open to you at this point. One is the Chapter XI reorganization, to be discussed in Chapter 26 on bankruptcy. Another is government lending agencies designed more or less specifically for the firm in temporary or reversible straits. The SBA offers direct loans (presently unavailable due to lack of funds) as well as bank loan guarantees for firms unable to meet normal bank lending standards. State or regional agencies (e.g., Massachusetts Business Development Corporation) make loans to faltering firms. Your chances with these people are best if you're a substantial employer, but let them judge that. Go see anybody whom you even suspect is in the economic development business. Your state legislator may be a good man to steer you to the right doors and help you to kick them open. If a federal program appears to have some glimmer of salvation, you should also keep your congressman or senator aware of your activities. Don't forget that they have a big stake in the economic welfare of their constituents.

For you, the entrepreneur, the toughest part of this whole business may be in keeping your own faith alive. With it, anything is possible (if improbable); without it, you won't be able to convince anybody. You may at times have to indulge in a little autohypnosis to keep on going, but a confident, enthusiastic, and optimistic attitude is essential —and contagious. You must evince the belief that the hurdle you confront is the last major one between the company and the Big Apple.

REFERENCES

1 / Hutchinson, G. S., *Why, When, and How To Go Public,* New York: Presidents Publishing House, 1970.

This offers prudent, if somewhat orthodox, advice and procedures for going public. Best book I've found on the subject.

2 / Sears, G. A., **"Public Offerings for Smaller Companies"**, *Harvard Business Review,* September–October, 1968.

3 / *A Summary of Financial Assistance Programs.* Washington, D.C.: Small Business Administration, 1966.

There may be a later edition. Lists a surprising number of government-backed financial assistance programs for small business, most of which are still around.

PART III

PEOPLE

16

people
in
small firms:
general
considerations

Youth gets together his materials to build a bridge to the moon, or perchance a palace or temple on earth, and, at length, the middle-aged man concludes to build a woodshed with them.

✢ HENRY DAVID THOREAU ✢

The most important resource of any company is its people. As an entrepreneur, one of your most important jobs for the next several years will be the recruiting, training, motivating, and, where necessary, thinning out of your staff. Much of your energy will be consumed with such issues as training new salesmen, creating compensation and incentive packages, struggling with rivalries and conflicts within your team, trying to maintain a creative climate, and getting rid of people who don't work out. To the extent that you are efficient and successful in these tasks, you will probably be efficient and successful in building your company.

THE FALLACY OF HIRING FOR FUTURE NEEDS

In Chapter 5 we addressed the issue of overspecification of partners in the fetal and start-up phases of the enterprise. The same general point can be made for any employee, however. You are doing a disservice to both the employee and the company to hire somebody who is over-qualified for the job at hand.

The practice of overhiring is sometimes justified by the argument that, while the employee's talents aren't needed now, in a year or two he will be fully utilized. Using this justification, many firms exploited the recent recession in hiring $20,000/year men to do junior engineering for $12,000—with very disappointing results for all concerned. Hiring an overqualified person can result in several problems:

1 / In hiring "the top person" for the job, you will normally be overpaying, relative to what it would otherwise cost to get the job done.

2 / If you take advantage of unusual market conditions to hire a person for less than his normal worth, you will invest money and effort in training him, only to lose him as soon as a normal job market returns.

3 / In the very early stages, before the company has significant substance, you will have to pay more in terms of salary, options, stock, and other nonsalary incentives to attract a top person than you will later.

4 / If the employee is from a larger company (which in all likelihood he is), he will be accustomed to staff, clerical help, substantial budgets, and other trappings of office. He may function poorly in the spartan environment you offer—or worse, persuade you to add the overheads long before you should.

5 / If he's bored by the detail and drudgery inherent in a new-company job, he may quit long before his talents are actually needed by the company.

As an entrepreneur, your responsibility is to survive the first couple of years—not to "build for the future" with people who won't be needed until Year Three. Therefore, match your hiring to the actual job as it will be for the next 1½–2 years. The future can take care of itself.

THE EMPLOYEE WHOSE JOB OUTGROWS HIM

In one version of *The Peter Principle*,[1] a man gets successive promotions until he reaches his "level of incompetence", after which he advances no further and prevents the further progress of the organization in his

---

[1] Apologies to Laurence J. Peter and Raymond Hull, authors of *The Peter Principle* (New York: William Morrow and Co., 1969).

area. In the new enterprise context, however, *The Peter Principle* works somewhat differently. Instead of the individual's being promoted up the pyramid, the pyramid grows under the individual. The resulting situation, however, is the same. In the new enterprise it is more serious, though, in that the person who does not grow with his job can effectively block the progress of the entire company. You don't *have* the option of working around him—you must usually get rid of him or subordinate him to a new manager from outside. Either can present some unpleasantness.

For example, assume you have hired a manufacturing manager who is hard-working, loyal, and extremely competent—as long as he only has about 25 employees whom he can oversee directly. He enjoys first-line contact, and trains and motivates workers beautifully. But now your organization has grown. You now have 100 workers and 3 foremen. Your old manufacturing manager, however, is not thriving on his success. He dislikes supervising foremen; he misses the direct contact with the workers, and feels that the foremen are doing a poor job of training and supervising them. Production is falling more or less permanently behind schedule, quality is slipping a bit, and fire drills and confrontations have begun to replace planning as a management method. What do you do now?

The simplest answer might be to get rid of the guy. However, he is a good man, a friend by now, and has been with the company virtually from start-up. He will walk out with some stock that can no longer motivate the performance of another employee. Moreover, he's well liked by the team, and his ejection could have a devastating effect on morale.

A second answer is to bring in a higher-power manufacturing manager, and make the old one a foreman under him. This might work, but the old manager is likely to feel humiliated by his demotion, and to resent the fact that he no longer reports directly to the president. These factors may undermine his efficiency greatly.

A third course is to create a sinecure (e.g., Vice President for Manufacturing Coordination), but this is costly and will arouse the resentment of everyone.

There is no correct answer to such a situation. Your best bet overall is likely to be to get rid of the guy, even though it's painful. At least, once it's over it will eventually be forgotten. If you keep him on, you may just be buying yourself a future of trouble and lost opportunity. Change the scenario a bit, and substitute chief engineer, controller, or sales manager for manufacturing manager, and you have a drama that occurs in just about every small company sooner or later.

TALENT VERSUS EXPERIENCE

A different consequence of the overhiring dilemma arises from the entrepreneur's own tendency toward insecurity in a new marketplace. It always seems like a surer bet to hire somebody who has been in the industry a while, who has a reasonable track record, etc. This applies with particular emphasis to hiring sales personnel. Your alternative, of course, is simply to hire a very good junior employee and hope that he will grow into the position quickly enough to compensate his lack of experience. If, of course, it were possible to hire someone with both talent *and* experience, the dilemma would never arise. However, in the general case you will be obliged to settle for one or the other.

If it comes to a showdown between talent and experience, you will always be better off to err on the side of talent. The older, more experienced hand may be ideal for some jobs. However, it is more often the case that in the new enterprise his experience becomes a liability rather than an asset. His previous success may have been a function of the market dominance of his former employer, or of an early product advantage, or of some market condition that no longer applies. To be effective, he may require a full product line, an applications engineering staff, a big ad budget, and a big-company reputation to back up product credibility. You will be unable to support him fully in any of these areas.

The junior person, on the other hand, will be out to make his mark. He will be willing to pour in the energy and time needed to develop *your* product, *your* market, *your* company. He will be more disposed to innovate and to work around the resource limitations inherent in the situation. Finally, even though there may be significant age difference between you, there is likely to be a much better impedance match between employee and president. Both will be in a learning experience. Both will be innovating and improvising. Both should be capable of taking a fresh look at what the competition is doing well and poorly, and at what the market really needs. To avoid creating a case of the blind leading the blind, both should be looking outside the company for some experienced guidance. This can come from directors, from the company godfather, from professional associations, or from elsewhere. Via this route, hiring a bright junior person can sometimes be much less risky for the company than taking on the man with "many years of experience".

MAINTAINING A CREATIVE ENVIRONMENT

Endless books, articles, and dissertations have been written on the problem of establishing and maintaining a climate of creativity in the business enterprise. A few of the better examples are to be found among the "References" to this chapter. However, most begin with the assumption that where creativity is concerned, the more the better. A few irreverent words on this subject may therefore be in order.

Creativity is to the organization what food is to an organism. With too little, it will anguish and die of malnutrition. With too much, it will become bloated, arteriosclerotic, immobile—and will also die. As with nourishment in organisms, there is a range of creativity that is somewhat near optimum for a given organization. Business enterprises vary drastically in their capacity to utilize creativity. An aerospace firm developing space-flight hardware, for example, inherently requires and consumes more ideas than a firm making plumbing supplies. In the former, the ratio of scientists and engineers to direct workers may be 1:1. In the latter it may be 1:1000 (which is not to imply that only scientists and engineers are creative, but merely to indicate a tendency).

In the earliest stages of your venture you will not be troubled with the need to strike this balance. Everyone on the team will be innovating, setting up their areas of functional responsibility, and trying to relate them to the needs of the company. Everyone is excited, working hard, and highly motivated. It is precisely this atmosphere of heady involvement, in fact, that permits you to attract still more first-class people. The excitement, involvement, and creativity substitute for the security of the larger employer.

However, as the orders begin to come in, as delivery pressure mounts, and as day-to-day operating problems begin to replace the yeasty excitement of a year ago, you will begin to confront the first real challenge: to maintain an atmosphere of creativity without overdoing it. Your methods for accomplishing this will of necessity change as the company expands in size and changes in character. In general, the larger you get, the harder the task will get.

In a creative environment, ideas are sincerely elicited, evaluated impartially, and implemented as warranted to prove themselves. There is an openness of communication, a minimum of perceptible hierarchy, and a willingness to suspend judgment of the ideas of others until they are fully explained and understood. There is a sharing of power among staff and a willingness to become involved in problem solution that, strictly speaking, falls outside one's range of immediate responsibility. There is recognition and perhaps tangible reward for the inventor (who thought up the idea) and the innovator (who implemented it).

At the opposite end of the spectrum, the noncreative environment is often characterized by authoritarian innovation from the top down; by an attitude among subordinates that says "I don't get paid to think about that"; by defensive tactics, not-invented-here attitudes, and contests to see who can shoot down the other fellow's idea first (perhaps in retaliation for the shooting down of one's own pet idea). There is little effort to elicit ideas and lack of recognition for even those whose ideas are implemented. Efforts to elicit ideas on a single problem in this environment are likely to be regarded as being manipulative.

We will not provide here a long checklist of all the things you can do to maintain a climate of creativity in your firm. The context and personalities dictate almost entirely what will work in a given organization. For hourly people, you may wish to try a suggestion system with cash awards. For professional personnel, try leaving your door open to everybody. Try brainstorming or synectic sessions for specific problems (e.g., new product definition). When an idea is implemented, make sure everybody knows about it. Try to keep criticism for lost sales, missed delivery dates, etc., to a low level—attack your problems, not your people. Try to keep creativity focused on real problems, and on solutions that are affordable and that can realistically be implemented.

The overcreative environment is occasionally found in technology companies—especially those trying to make a transition from consulting or R & D to products. There is positive competition to see who can be the most "creative"; emphasis on generation of myriads of ideas rather than on evaluation and practical implementation makes it impossible for anyone to focus on any common objective. The resources of the company become dissipated in the pursuit of too many ideas and as a consequence, none gets carried to complete fruition.

REFERENCES

1 / Carlin, G. S., *How To Motivate and Persuade People.* West Nyack, New York: Parker Publishing Co., 1964.

Practical, usable ideas on the entrepreneur's No. 1 problem: moti-

vating and persuading employees, customers, suppliers, and financial backers.

2 / Taylor, Jack W., *How To Select and Develop Leaders.* New York: McGraw-Hill Co., 1962.

This is a fairly good, pragmatic guide to identifying and developing leadership and other talents in your associates and employees.

17

acquiring
and
divesting
people

Hell is—other people!

❖ JEAN PAUL SARTRE *❖*

A considerable amount of your personal energies during the first several quarters of operation will be consumed by the establishment and implementation of policies and practices for dealing with personnel. Acquiring and divesting people can be considered among the most highly entrepreneurial of your tasks. To the extent that it is done reasonably well, every other task in the new enterprise will be just that much easier to do. This chapter focuses on some practical considerations to help you do the job well.

COMPENSATION PACKAGES

Beyond the privilege of working in your exciting, creative environment, your prospective employee will be looking for a few other things, including salary, vacation, holidays, sick leave, insurance, stock purchase plans, profit sharing, commissions, bonuses, and perhaps education payment. A few words may be in order on each.

✠ SALARY

In establishing an offering salary, do not attempt to induce the employee to accept a salary lower than his market worth by relying on the glamour of the new enterprise or stressing vague future stock benefits. Pay each person his full market worth; then use the other intangibles, stock, etc., to get twice the effort from him for the money. It's OK for the founding group to operate on partial salaries for a while to conserve cash or enhance operating profits, but it's totally unrealistic to expect a first-rate employee to come on board for less than his worth. Various state manpower surveys, as well as personnel managers of other firms, can give you guidance in setting salaries, if you're in doubt.

✠ VACATION, SICK LEAVE, HOLIDAYS

Your vacation policy will probably be dictated for you by the practices of the region you're in. At the outset, forget about plans that increase the vacation time as tenure reaches 10, then 20 years. Your principal decision in this regard will be whether to have a two-week plant shutdown each year, or whether to permit staggered or partial vacations for your people. Holidays and sick leave policies will also be dictated to a large degree by the practices of the area in which you're recruiting.

✠ INSURANCE

The immediate need is for some form of group medical coverage, just as soon as you qualify. It is much better to start at least a modest plan with high deductibles and minimal benefits than risk having anybody wiped out financially by medical costs. Start out with the company paying only a fraction of the cost; then build up this fraction (with suitable fanfare) as the company matures. Many medical packages can be supplemented with a small amount of life insurance (say, one year's salary). Such term life insurance is rather inexpensive and should also be considered since many of your nonprofessional people may have no other personal life insurance.

✠ STOCK PURCHASE PLANS

Where small companies are concerned, everybody wants a piece of the action. Since the subject is going to come up virtually every time you interview somebody for a professional job, it is desirable to have the policy for nonfounder stock purchase worked out and committed to writing in advance of recruiting. Stock purchase and stock option plans abound, but they have only one purpose: to motivate *those within the company*. They act as an incentive to those who are working to earn them; they act as a double incentive to those who already have them. Your attorney will be able to review for you the several types of restricted stock option plans with their business benefits and tax characteristics.

Try to design a plan sufficiently flexible that you will not have to abandon it in the first exceptional situation. Make sure that each new employee "earns" his way in—don't include stock as part of an initial offer.

Be concrete on the subject of stock. Don't make vague promises that you would be unwilling to put in writing, and be certain that stock purchase privileges are related to performance in an agreed-upon way.

✠ PROFIT SHARING PLAN

Forget it. It will be a long time before there are any profits to share. It will be longer yet before there is excess cash to pay out on a plan. Therefore, its existence will only create disappointed employees.

✠ BONUSES AND COMMISSIONS

Except for salesmen's commissions, there isn't much benefit to a bonus plan in the new enterprise. Even if the employee performs dazzlingly, his very success may create additional growth that in turn absorbs the cash to pay bonuses. In the case of salesmen, however, the commission incentive is usually what gets them out of bed in the morning. Eliminate it at your peril.

✠ EDUCATION PAYMENTS

In a new company, especially a technology venture, some of your employees will be disposed toward continuing their education in work-related fields. Even small companies find that the cost of partial or complete tuition reimbursement is often justified as a recruiting incentive and as a way of upgrading the abilities of people on the job. In some geographic areas it may in fact be a virtual competitive necessity.

✠ OTHER RANDOM BENEFITS

You may find that certain other employee benefits may be very popular without adding much actual cost. These include vesting savings plans, credit unions, sports, parties, luncheon facilities, etc. It is very easy to go overboard in this department—especially when you, the boss, are expected to show up for these activities. However, don't underestimate the importance of these things to your people, especially those in the nonprofessional ranks of the company. In this area, it is best for everyone if the initiatives come from the employees themselves.

RECRUITING

Now you have it all together: a hot company, a creative working environment, and a well-thought-out compensation package. Now, how do you find a prospective employee?

Your tactics in finding good prospects will, of course, depend upon the job to be filled. However, try to exercise the lowest-cost sources first, as recruitment *can* be very costly. The following are places you can advertise for employees, in order of ascending cost:

1 / *School placement bureaus.* Colleges, technical institutes, secretarial schools, and vocational high schools all maintain offices for the placement of both new graduates and alumni changing jobs. If you're looking for technicians, don't overlook Job Corps and similar community- or government-sponsored training and retraining programs.

2 / *Your own company.* A conspicuous sign on your plant for nonprofessional help may net you some candidates, and it is an indication of company growth to outsiders.

3 / *Professional societies.* A low-cost notice in the society journal or newsletter, or on the bulletin board at the annual convention can net you many prospective employees. There are also, at time of writing, some loose federations of unemployed technical professionals, which may become permanent placement agencies.

4 / *Government employment agencies.* State governments offer placement services for both professional and nonprofessional people, at no cost to users.

5 / *Firms known to be laying off.* The placement directors of such firms will be glad to hear from you although, of course, you must realize that the best employees are not the first to be let go. This nonetheless can be a good source of leads.

6 / *Newspaper advertising.* This is not inexpensive, especially when pursued in national publications such as the *Wall Street Journal, Electronic News,* etc. However, it can be quite effective, since the newspaper is the first place a man looking around will inquire—it costs him nothing in terms of effort or commitment to anybody to look at the paper. Even if he's still employed, your ad may just spark the desire to make a change. You need not be splashy with your ad, but it should be large enough to convey a reasonable amount of information and the impression of substance.

7 / *Personnel agencies.* Private agencies vary in quality from lousy to excellent. They also vary in the types of personnel they are effective at recruiting. One way in which they are alike, however, is expense. None is cheap. For a secretary, the fee might be two weeks salary; for an engineer or a manager, it could be 1–2 months salary. As soon as you run an advertisement in the papers, you may be besieged by agencies that have "just the person for the job". Your best strategy is to keep them at bay until you're sure the other sources are not going to come through for you. Then, do some inquiring and visit the agency. Some will engage in some limited search in your behalf—others will just fire off résumés of everybody in their files. Instead of a mechanical engineer, you may end up reading the résumé of a locomotive engineer!

8 / *Personnel search agencies.* Now you're talking about real money. The professional head-hunters usually don't operate on a results basis—they generally want a retainer fee, and maybe a commission, too. They are normally employed by larger companies in filling the higher management posts. The head-hunter tries to find the top three or four men in the field; then approaches them discreetly in behalf of his unnamed client. This probably is not a recruitment channel available or appropriate to most new ventures.

INTERVIEWING

Once you've lavished money, energy, and calendar time in trying to find suitable candidates, it's a pity to blow it all in the interview. Yet this is precisely what happens in an unnecessarily large number of instances. The prospect gets rejected for the wrong reasons, gets hired for the wrong reasons, or gets an offer that he does not accept.

Employment interviewing is a subject about which a good deal is known. A couple of better references on the subject are listed at the end of this chapter. It is probably well worth your while as a company president to spend a long evening reading some of this material and developing a more or less formal interview strategy. By so doing, you'll learn a lot more about the candidate, you'll avoid missing any critical areas, and you'll do a much better job of selling your company to the person you want.

THE NEW EMPLOYEE

In addition to the normal procedural details of signing up for health plans, withholding, etc., your new employee should be asked to sign an Invention Disclosure Agreement. If this is not among the first things he signs coming on board, you will have great difficulty in getting him to sign it later—especially if he has been assisting in your firm's R & D function and has made some valuable discovery! One of the first actions of the start-up company president should be to work with the attorney and develop a suitable agreement of this type for all appropriate employees. To delay it is an invitation to downstream problems.

Although few new companies have a formal training program of any sort, there should be a single individual responsible for the training of the new recruit, and you should commit to writing the exact steps that will be taken to integrate the new employee into the organization. For a production person, this might include familiarization wth company rules, policies, production methods, workmanship standards, and related information. For a new controller, it would perhaps include exposure to the operating business plan, familiarization with the existing accounting system and financial history of the company, and orientation with regard to major customers and vendors.

In small companies, it is often difficult to write satisfactory job descriptions because people tend, after a while in the firm, to structure the job to suit themselves. One of the strengths of the small business environment is, in fact, the ability to accommodate itself to the skills and interests of the individual employees, to a degree not possible in the large firm. Nonetheless, it is very necessary that the president be sure that a job description is in fact written for *every* position to be filled. This description, in addition to describing the job to be done immediately, should describe the directions of growth, added responsibilities, and functions that might be added to the job. It should specify the minimum, desired, and optimal qualifications that a successful candidate would have. Although it may need modification in the future, such a description is absolutely necessary for several obvious reasons. It helps management decide if an employee is needed at all (a question that sometimes doesn't even get asked!), how to budget for the job, how to advertise the position, and how to communicate about the job with the candidate. It also helps to establish the performance criteria for the new employee.

DIVESTING PEOPLE

One of the least pleasant experiences of the entrepreneur is getting rid of people who (a) haven't performed as expected, or (b) must be jettisoned in a company cutback. Most entrepreneurs encounter the first case fairly often, and the second at least once in the first 2–4 years of operation. These two cases are sufficiently different to warrant some individual comment.

✠ THE LOW PERFORMER

Most entrepreneurs seem to put off the inevitable long past the point where it is obvious that a particular person is not going to hack it. There may be pressure to "Give Joe just one more chance." There may be extenuating circumstances that could "explain" his lack of performance. There may be some areas in which he's doing a good job, and with some more help he may improve. *Forget it.* You're only kidding yourself. You are telling yourself that you're being humane, being fair. However, in reality, you *know* he isn't going to make it. So you're only sparing yourself the discomfort of acting.

When you do act, it should be decisive and clean. Repeated warnings, probationary periods, etc., probably just prolong the agony. If a visibly low performer stays around, you damage the morale of the entire team and, worse, handicap the functional area for which he is responsible. Give the employee his notice (usually two weeks), but tell him that he should use the two weeks to look for a job. (You do *not* want a person who's been fired around the plant or office for two weeks.)

In your termination interview, try to be fair. Tell him why he's being terminated. Spare the soft soap (e.g., "You're just overqualified for our job"). Help him to understand where he went off the track, so he can find a more appropriate opening or operational method in the future. He won't be grateful, but at least he won't spend the rest of his life wondering why he was fired. To help ease the transition, you should make sure that his medical insurance is extended to cover his interval of unemployment. You should steer him toward state agencies for personnel placement, unemployment insurance, and other benefits to which he may be entitled. You may be able to suggest companies of which you are aware that are hiring, or job training programs which can help him in his areas of weakness. In short, by helping to make the best of his opportunities, you are doing him a much bigger favor than you would by keeping him on for a few more months.

✠ THE CUTBACK

This situation is much worse than being faced with the low performer. The company has hit some rough sailing—maybe a business recession. Now you are obliged to terminate not only some marginal people but also some people who have been doing a good job. And you may be putting them on the street at the very time that other firms are laying off, too (as, for example, during our "recession" of 1969–1970). This is the sort of thing ulcers are made of.

Just deciding who's going to be thrown out of the boat to lighten the load is a difficult process. You should probably not even discuss it with your partners in the office, since rumors have a way of starting—particularly when business conditions have everyone apprehensive anyway—and undermining morale and performance, thereby worsening a bad situation. Your main job is to make the cuts without demolishing the morale of the remaining troops. This is a challenge, to say the least.

While emerging business conditions may make this impossible, you should strive to make your total cut at once, as opposed to a few every Friday. The effect will be stunning, but will challenge those remaining to close ranks and try to get the job done without the people who have gone. In the other case, everyone will be wondering all week if he's going to be the next to go. Your less effective people will start digging in, and mounting defensive tactics. Your better people will start looking around, and some of them may find other jobs and leave. The net result is that the initiative is taken away from you, the morale of the team is undermined, and the best people leave or wish they could. Make your bloodletting as clean, brief, and complete as possible.

You can take the same steps to assist the victims as you did for the low performer. In addition, you may wish to call up the personnel directors of other employers in the area, and let them know who is available. If the cutbacks are largely regional, you may be able to make contact with firms in other areas, too. If the cutback is the result of a severe recession, there may be special agencies established for counseling job-seekers, to which you can refer the terminated employee.

In all, this is not a happy experience for entrepreneurs. The fact that almost everybody has to face it sooner or later may be some consolation.

A NOTE ON THE PERSONNEL FUNCTION

In the small company the function of personnel management tends to be an orphan for quite a while. Just the management of employee records, withholding statements, pre-employment medical exams, coordination of health insurance claims, etc., can be a substantial burden. If you're very lucky, you may find a secretary or accounting clerk whose inclinations tend in this direction. If so, give that employee the job, and fill in with other work. The person who handles time sheets and payroll may be a good choice for the responsibility to prevent wide dispersion of salary data or other personal information. Just be sure somebody is responsible for the whole job.

Fairly early in your growth, you should develop a Personnel Manual, dealing with every phase of employment, including rules, policies, benefits, patent policy, etc. The easiest way to do a good job on this is to get somebody else's, and edit it to suit your needs.

REFERENCES

1 / Black, J. M., *How To Get Results from Interviewing.* New York: McGraw-Hill Co., 1970.

This is a very practical guide to planning interview strategy. Covers specific cases such as hiring, promotion, discipline, exit.

2 / Hariton, Theodore, *Interview: The Executive's Guide to Selecting the Right Personnel.* New York: Hastings House Publishing Co., 1970.

This is an excellent guide to hiring interviews. Very practical, incorporating suggested forms and interview formats. Must reading.

3 / O'Neal, F. H., *Expulsion or Oppression of Business Associates: Squeeze-Outs in Small Enterprises.* Durham, N.C.: Duke University Press, 1961.

One of the few books on a delicate topic: how to be a successful squeezer, or avoid being a squeezee.

4 / Peter, Laurence J., and Raymond Hull, *The Peter Principle.* New York: William Morrow and Co., 1969.

How to tell when you've reached your level of incompetence.

PART IV

MARKETING

18

selling

Nothing happens until you get a purchase order.

❊ Anonymous ❊

A salesman is got to dream, boy. It comes with the territory.

❊ Willy Loman ❊

Selling is the central activity of the business enterprise. If you have this ability, you will always be able to find a useful product to sell; if you have only the ability to engineer or produce products, you may be a bankruptcy looking for someplace to happen. The value of selling is often driven home to manufacturers in a dismaying but forceful way: The firm selling its output through an independent sales organization (e.g., Sears, Roebuck; Radio Shack; J. C. Whitney) usually at some point realizes that the selling organization is making much higher gross margins and net profits than the manufacturer. Is this unfair, or merely the marketplace placing a proper valuation on the function of selling?

IMAGE VERSUS REALITY

In the very earliest phases of company growth, there will be a great divergence between the image you wish to project to the market and the actual substance to back it up. It is doubly important at this phase that your actions, statements, literature, and advertising do not bespeak an amateur, unprofessional, or fly-by-night operation. We have addressed this issue in Chapter 6 with regard to the preparation of initial literature. However, it applies to other phases of your selling efforts as well.

Most of your customers and prospective customers will never see more of your company than your salesmen, advertisements, documentation, and products. Most will not see your plant, your beautiful lobby and conference room, your spiffy shop, etc. This is fortunate. Remember, although the plant may be a source of great pride to you, it still looks pretty rinky-dink to a visitor from IBM who is considering your product. Be sure that the things he *does* see are not rinky-dink. You want him to have the impression of a solid, growing company that is going to be around to back up its products, to supply his future needs, to be a source of pride if your product is included in his. Remember that the buyer feels his neck is out a mile if he's purchasing from you, rather than from your much larger competitor. Poor literature, clumsy presentation, improvised product documentation, etc., only add to his inherent sense of uneasiness. Do these things *right* even if it costs a few dollars. They are as much a part of your product as the hardware itself.

✠ LITERATURE

Be sure that it looks at least as good as your competitors'. List a variety of models, options, accessories, even if they aren't exactly ready for delivery yet.

✠ PRICING AND PRICE LISTS

Try to stay within the conventions of the industry, at least initially. You should use the same methods of discounting, commercial terms, etc., that your customer is accustomed to. Don't try to innovate.

✠ ADVERTISING

If you can't justify the cost of competing at a respectable level with your competitors, consider deferring magazine advertising altogether. Or use the occasional big ad with less frequency, hitting the annual Buyer's Guide issues, etc. Try some innovation instead. Use some direct mailings, telephone solicitation, recorded casette pitches, demonstration van, etc. Think of ways to make yourself appear more *innovative* than your competitor.

✠ PROMOTION

This is the area in which you can shine, at reasonable cost. Create lots of press releases on new products, new developments, new building, new contracts, new overseas agents, etc. Write articles for the trade press, the popular press. Present papers at the society meetings. Hold application seminars at strategic locations around the country, and invite the press as well as customers. You can come off looking much better than a less ambitious competitor.

✠ PRODUCT DOCUMENTATION

Be sure that your operation manuals, instruction sheets, maintenance manuals, etc., are up to the standards of the industry. Nothing makes an expensive, engineered product look sillier than sending a blueprint of a circuit diagram instead of a professional-looking manual. This documentation is *part* of your product. Treat it accordingly.

ADVERTISING AGENCIES

It is probable that, at the outset at least, you do not need a regular ad agency. What you *do* need is, ideally, a part-time artist and layout person who has worked for an agency. You need good advice and good art in designing letterheads, logo, literature, and perhaps occasional ads. Such a person can also be helpful in the design of trade show exhibits, visual aids for speeches, etc. Find the right person for this role, and you will save yourself thousands of dollars and untold aggravation.

As your company progresses and an advertising agency appears justified, do some shopping. Some will want to take over your whole marketing effort. Others will want to push for big, commissionable magazine ad budgets. Some will want to give you a whole new image. What you want is a small, hard-working, cost-conscious, and practical agency that will do what *you* want at a price you can afford. And even then, you will want to keep some of the work with your part-time artist—especially literature, which requires some continuity of appearance.

Your agency may also wish to handle your public relations and publicity. This is seldom a good idea because of the fact that editors and reporters like to talk to the president. Moreover, product releases and stories written by you will be much easier to generate, cheaper, and better in quality. Just be sure it gets done.

PRICING

The pricing of your product offers opportunity for many commonly committed errors. Here are some of them:

1 / Basing pricing on cost of manufacture, rather than on value to customer. Engineers are particularly prone to price new products on "cost-plus-overhead-plus-profit" formulas, neglecting the fact that the product may be worth far more to the user.

2 / Basing pricing on present low overheads, rather than projecting into the future to see how the overheads will grow.

3 / Failing to include allowance for warranty costs, future servicing, design amortization, application engineering, cost of capital, etc.

4 / Assuming that because you are the newest firm in the field, you must of necessity have the lowest prices to get established. Your product strategy might, on the contrary, be to build the Cadillac of the industry, leaving the larger volume sales to other competitors.

5 / Failing to even estimate the demand elasticity for the the product. How much *would* sales volume increase if prices were lowered 10 percent or 20 percent? Is your product unique enough to command a premium over others if you increase the price? Finally, what is your *maximum-profit* volume, given the price–volume curve?

6 / Failing to employ some version of *market skimming*— starting off with a high price until demand is saturated, then lowering the price gradually. This way, in theory at least, each person gets a chance to pay his maximum price for the product.

Adequate high pricing has its perils for the new company, like any other prescriptive measure. For example, if your prices and profits are outrageously high, you may be inviting early competition that would not otherwise enter your market. Remember, too, that your late-comer competitor will have little of the market research, product development, and lost-motion cost that you incurred, so he will be in a position to cut your prices substantially.

This factor notwithstanding, the burden of proof is definitely on the low, rather than the high, price in a new business venture. It's a lot easier to lower them if you err on the high side than the other way around.

CONTINUOUS MARKET RESEARCH

In Chapter 4 "Measuring the Need", we treated the development of a first-cut market research project that would have a specific result for fund-raising efforts. However, market research does not end there; it is a more or less continuous process in which the president is subliminally engaged all the time. Observing needs that the company can fill; scanning the literature for new developments, pricing trends, competitor actions, availability of customer funding, acquisition of customers or competitors—these are all ways in which the company president must tune himself to signals from the marketplace. In addition, the company may be engaged in a series of more or less continuous formal market analyses for products you are contemplating introducing. Scanning *all* the relevant periodicals; travelling to visit customers and working with salesmen; attending trade shows, professional meetings, trade fairs, etc., are the principal means of staying open to market intelligence. Do not permit your new sales manager to isolate you from contact with customers, with salesmen, or with reps. These are your communication lines with reality. Guard them jealously.

BUILDING A REP ORGANIZATION

Independent sales representatives are the marketing backbone of many industries. For present purposes, let us also include in this category agents, discount dealers, jobbers, and others who sell your products without actually being on your payroll.

Unless reps are completely unsuitable or unavailable for your product, you will wish to consider using them as your initial sales organization. The advantages and disadvantages of reps, as opposed to direct salesmen, are as follows:

Advantages

1 / The rep requires no fixed cost. Reps get paid only when they make a sale. Dealers who stock your product pay in advance as a rule. Both effects greatly enhance the cash flow and minimize the capital requirements of the small company.

2 / The rep has knowledge of territory and prospective customers.

3 / The rep may have several reasons to visit a prospect (i.e., several product lines of interest). Thus, his frequency of contact per customer may be higher than that of your own salesman.

4 / The rep may have special capabilities to offer you or your customer, such as installation and repair services, application engineering, stocking against special needs, etc.

5 / The rep may be conducting his own advertising and promotion efforts and may be willing to share in the costs of advertising your product in his territory.

Disadvantages

1 / Most reps have a lot of lines but devote most of their energies to selling one or two established, bread-and-butter lines.

2 / A rep may not push even a successful line too hard for fear that the company may decide to replace him with a direct salesman at lower total cost.

3 / Many reps can function effectively only as finders, and require a great deal of factory personnel support to actually close a sale.

4 / Reps are difficult to monitor, train, and motivate. The successful reps may lack the time, the unsuccessful ones the inclination, to work intensively with you in building up your market.

Despite the disadvantages, however, reps give the young company a running start on the market. They represent the only way that many small firms can even consider establishing national marketing in the first year of operation.

✠ IDENTIFYING AND RECRUITING REPS

There are several more or less orthodox ways to identify possible reps. The first is through searching in trade directories. Although these are often out of date, due to frequent changes of line (and identity) among reps, directories can tell you what reps are in a given area, what types of lines they handle, what types of customers they service. You may be able to find the reps of your competitor or of a maker of complementary products. Identification can also proceed through associations of reps and dealers. These may be national (e.g., the Electronic Representatives Association) or local rep organizations. Chambers of commerce, at both city and state levels, often maintain lists of reps and agents as well. Also, if you can identify a friendly manufacturer of complementary products, you can simply call his sales manager and inquire whether they have a good rep in Dayton. He may welcome the chance to pool data with you.

Recruitment normally begins with a phone call or a letter outlining your product, your company, your prospects in the rep's territory. If he's not interested, he can often tell you who else to talk to. If he is, your next step is a visit to his office. Ideally, this visit should include scheduling two or three actual sales calls to prospective customers in the territory. This gives you some opportunity to assess his contacts and his selling approach, while at the same time *he* can calibrate the customers' interest in your product. Since you've gone to the trouble and expense of visiting the rep, don't leave without making the direct sales calls. If he seems reluctant, this may tell you something, too.

Before signing up a rep, you should both have some understanding as to the range of sales volume that you might realistically expect from the territory for the ensuing several quarters. He may be a much better judge of this than you are. You will also want a signed contract. These are normally quite informal; reps and other sales managers are a good source of samples. Finally, you should check him out with his other principals as well as with some of his local customers.

✠ SUCCEEDING WITH REPS

Recruiting a rep organization is one thing; making it a success is another. The initial blush of enthusiasm wanes quickly on both sides, as the hard digging of actually building sales begins in earnest. You both are destined for a number of disappointments. You may think he personally flubbed the biggest contract you've gone after yet. He may seem to be always and forever requesting some nonstandard product modification or unrealistic price concession. *He* may think *you're* an idiot because you wouldn't promise to deliver fast enough to get the order. He will probably consider your company unresponsive to market needs. In short, there are many more opportunities for the relationship to run awry than to run smoothly. The smart president will anticipate this and work hard to make the relationship work. Here are some things you can do:

1 / *Contact every rep once a week,* by phone or in person, even if there's no pressing reason to do so. Ask what's going on and how you can help.

2 / *Supply plenty of sales leads for him to follow.* Don't oblige him to go sit in the lobby and talk cold to purchasing managers (most reps won't anyway). This is one important function of your advertising/promotion program.

3 / *Give him a decent sales manual.* Don't force him to rely only on your data sheets and price lists. Include applications notes, competitive comparisons, and glossy product photos, including "inside the box" shots. Give him sales arguments. List the possible objections and the counter-arguments. Give him a list of happy users for customer reference. Provide reprints of impressive journal articles. In short, give him all the ammunition you can think of—he's your man in the trenches and he needs it.

4 / *Try gimmicks to keep reps informed and keep their attention.* A newsletter, describing new company developments, product of the month, *rep* of the month, sales volumes, etc., can be inexpensive and effective. Send him copies of all the press release packages you send the press. Try sales contests, prizes, incentives, "this-month-only" discounts, or double commissions on specific products you want to push. Let them know you're alive. Remember, you're competing for their time with all their other principal companies.

5 / *Get someone out in the field to work with them.* Be ready to jump on a plane when the call for help comes. Be prepared to close the first few orders yourself. Support him when he needs support. Take an occasional swing through the country and work with each rep. Get on a first-name basis with all his salesmen.

6 / *Follow up your sales leads.* Keep your own lists, and find out politely but firmly what he's done on each of them. Let him know you appreciate his follow-up and are interested in the unsuccessful quotations as well as the hot ones.

7 / *Pay your commissions on time.* Nothing throws cold water on a rep relationship faster than unpaid commissions. Some companies, when they get in a cash crunch, include commissions in the deferrable expense category. You could not make a bigger mistake. Loss of a key rep can cripple a company for many quarters. You'd be better off laying off a few plant personnel than risk the dissolution of your sales organization.

8 / *Have an annual sales meeting at the plant.* Put on the dog a bit. Let the reps pay their transportation, but you pay hotels and meals. Let them meet all your people and see your plant. Have some sales sessions, some technical sessions, some gripe sessions. Work on specific problems individually. In short, let them become a part of your team—this, basically, is what a good rep *wants* to do.

9 / *Deliver on your product promises.* Nothing gets the rep in hot water faster than late delivery, improper operation, balky warranty service, or other forms of bungling by the factory. He *must believe* that the product he sells is going to be the answer to his customer's prayers. If he believes anything less, your chances of getting sales are seriously compromised. If, as is often the case in a small company, the rep has a very souring experience with you, you may want to get rid of him, even though he has not resigned. Once his confidence has been damaged, it may not be possible by 10 successes to restore it.

Remember, he needs the long-term goodwill of those big firms in his territory a whole lot more than he needs you. When the chips are down, he'll be forced to

side with his customer and find a better source for the
product they want.

10 / *Try to avoid "house" accounts.* Nothing is more de-
moralizing to a rep, even if he initially agreed to it, than
to see large shipments going into his territory without
commission to him. Even if he understands it, he will
never appreciate it—especially if it's a company he has
to call on for other principals anyway. On your part, it
may be tempting to exclude one fat customer you've
already developed on your own from the first rep that
comes along. A reasonable compromise may be to offer
the rep the house account as soon as his volume from
customers passes an agreed-upon target—say, $200,000.
Then he has a great incentive, and you are not risking
handing over a commission check each month to a do-
nothing rep. Or, some would argue, you want ideally to
give the rep enough volume at the outset to make your
line one of his most important—another way to command a major portion of his energies.

BEYOND REPS

It is commonly believed that the direct sales force is always the best way
to sell. Salaried salesmen are, it is argued, easier to control and motivate,
have no conflicting loyalties, are able to spend full time on your product,
and, when volume passes breakeven versus reps, are cheaper. These are
persuasive arguments. However, there are many companies with the volume, cash flow, and profits to sustain direct sales forces that stay with reps
exclusively, and there are many more who use a mixture of reps and
salesmen. So the jury is still out on this question. Or, more accurately,
there is a profit-maximizing mix in each case, depending upon the product, rep quality, market characteristics, and other variables. For this reason you should carefully assess the question of whether to replace all reps
as soon as possible with direct men. It is just possible that that nice breakeven volume may follow your old rep to your competitor's organization.

A realistic intermediate step is the establishment of regional offices,
each a one-man operation initially, charged with coordinating sales and
service for a specified territory. The regional manager can then work

directly with your reps in the territory, recruit and train his own reps, or, perhaps, handle some of the territory on a direct sales basis himself. Through this route, your move toward national marketing is advanced one large step further without foreclosing *any* options. Finally, when and if the time comes for additional direct salesmen, you have the framework in existence for their deployment and supervision.

YOUR JOB AS CHEERLEADER

As Napoleon Bonaparte observed, an army marches on its stomach. In precisely the same sense, a sales organization marches on its heart (or whatever other organ is used to store enthusiasm and morale). *You*—nobody else—are the sparkplug to whom everyone is looking for the zeal, the confidence, the incentive to get out of bed in the morning and face some hostile customers, traffic jams, a lobbyful of competitors, and the various snarl-ups that enrich the salesman's day. You are permanent cheerleader, morale officer, and chaplain rolled up in one. You must be accessible to reps, salesmen, and regional managers. You must show them that *sales*—not engineering, not accounting, not manufacturing—comes first in your outfit.

You must be willing to put your hand in the fire occasionally to add conviction to your rhetoric. You're the one who has to whip up enthusiasm for the new product, the new lower prices, the new demonstrator van. You're the one who has to head off delivery trouble, take over negotiations with problem customers, authorize special concessions to meet competition. Likewise, you are the one who must set the sales goals and enlist the commitment of all concerned with reaching those goals. You're the one responsible for seeing that the successful salesman or rep receives more than a paycheck or a commission check—that he also receives recognition from everyone in your organization—or, if warranted, a cordial kick in the tailfeathers. Salesmen are supposed to be self-starters, but it is nevertheless incumbent on you to be sure that the ignition key gets turned.

SELLING CAN BE LEARNED

Even the entrepreneur who is not a great natural salesman can learn a good deal about the art of selling without long costly trial-and-error education. Much is known about selling since people have been doing it for so long. Regardless of the market you serve, it is likely that there exists some sales course, weekend workshop, or seminar related more or less directly to your situation. These may be run by colleges, by the SBA, by the American Marketing Association chapter, by the local representatives association, etc. It is not beneath your dignity to enroll in such a course, or even to insist that your salesmen or partners do also. It is almost certain that you will gain some different perspective, insight, and usable ideas from the experience, as well as getting a chance to meet other sales people with problems comparable to your own.

You can also learn a good deal by studying the marketing methods of companies that have been successful, and from talking to their executives to gain some understanding of *why* they did what they did. The president of another growing firm, perhaps a stage or two ahead of your own, can be a good sounding board for marketing and other ideas.

CONVENTIONAL WISDOM ⟵ ➡ REALITY

Sell, sell, sell.   ***Sell, sell, sell.***

REFERENCES

1 /   Haas, K. B., and J. W. Ernest, **Creative Salesmanship: Understanding Essentials.** Beverly Hills, Calif.: The Glencoe Press, 1969.

This is a practical though academically respectable treatment of the entire topic of selling. It gives a particularly good treatment of buyer psychology and closing techniques.

2 /   Kotler, Philip, **Marketing Management: Analysis, Planning, and Control.** 2nd ed. Englewood Cliffs, N.J.: Prentice-Hall, Inc., 1972.

Despite the ponderous title, a very good basic marketing text covering each phase clearly and completely. Could be considered a reference work for the new president.

3 /   DeVoe, Merril, **How To Tailor Your Sales Organization to Your Markets.** Englewood Cliffs, N.J.: Prentice-Hall, 1964.

Very pragmatic, how-to-do-it information on organizing, recruiting, and motivating a sales team. Very good.

4 / Steinkamp, W. H., *How To Sell and Market Industrial Products.* Philadelphia: Chilton Book Co., 1970.

Similar in level and competence to No. 3, but focused on the industrial product.

5 / Levitt, Theodore, *The Marketing Mode—Pathways to Corporate Growth.* New York: McGraw-Hill Inc., 1969.

A long essay on marketing innovative products, by one of the most innovative marketing minds on the American scene.

6 / Gisser, P., *Launching the New Industrial Product.* New York: American Management Association, 1972.

This is brief and very practical, although directed more toward the established firm. It will tell you how you should do it, if you had the people, money, and established market momentum.

7 / Roth, C .B., *Treasury of Sure-Fire Selling Tips.* Englewood Cliffs, N.J.: Prentice-Hall, Inc., 1960.

This is a typical specimen of the pep-rally, "yes you can" school of literature for salesmen. May give you some ideas on training sales men to plan sales calls, and follow them up for maximum effect.

19

the

customer

It is naught, it is naught, saith the buyer: but when he is gone his way, then he boasteth.

❋ PROVERBS 20:14 ❋

The customer is, by definition, someone who needs what you can supply. He is the only reason for the existence of your business. Your greatest challenge will be to identify him, analyze his needs, and satisfy his requirements.

IDENTIFYING CUSTOMERS

Before your business plan was even put to bed, you had a list of prospective customers for your product. These were people whom you had surveyed, people known to be buying similar products, and people surmised to require your product. Now, however, you are in the marketplace, have rung all those doorbells, and have closed a few sales. What now? To build up a dynamic list of prospective, qualified customers is a big job. To keep it current and to keep the deadbeats off it is a bigger job yet. Among your tools will be:

1 / *Leads from advertising.* Readers' service ("bingo") card replies require further qualification, via return mail or phone contact with respondents. Direct letter replies and telephone contacts originating from advertising are among your best leads. Returns from direct mail campaigns are likely to be of higher quality, especially if the respondent must supply some data on his needs.

2 / *Leads from trade shows.* These may be readily qualified on the spot by the employee who talked to the prospect. The prospect has also had the advantage, in most cases, of having seen actual hardware at the show, further qualifying himself.

3 / *Leads from trade directories, etc.* If your product is bought mainly by hospitals with intensive care units, you can readily find most of your prospects in a directory. If it is bought by people who own sports cars, you probably can't. Between these extremes lie many classes of customers who can often be reached and qualified by mail, through lists extracted from trade directories.

4 / *Personal knowledge of reps and employees.* This may be among your most valuable sources of suspects because it has already been pre-screened.

5 / *Self-identification.* The *Commerce Business Daily*, advertisements soliciting proposals, form letters sent to suppliers, and government solicitations from firms on bidders' lists are some examples of this.

6 / *Leads from "data bases".* This is similar to the directory approach, but may permit greater pinpointing starting from a bigger sample. For example, the Dun & Bradstreet tapes might permit you to do a direct mailing to every firm performing ferrous casting operations with over 50 employees in the eastern half of the United States.

As your list of prospects grows, it can become a mailing list for direct mailing pieces, company announcements, newsletters, new literature, and price lists. Try to reach your list on a regular (say, monthly) basis, just as you try to contact each rep weekly. Make it a habit to let them hear from you. Be sure that the reps have all the names for their territory, so they can follow through. Try to keep the list in two sections: the mass list and the "top 100". Keep it current. Make its maintenance the special responsibility of one person in the company.

ANALYZING CUSTOMER NEEDS

In some businesses (e.g., manufacturing ball bearings) the customer's requirements are rather straightforward (he needs ball bearings). In other cases, however, it isn't so easy. In most capital equipment decisions, for example, there may be several equally feasible definitions of need. If a customer wishes, for example, to improve his accounting procedures, he may "need" a computer, or a time-sharing service, or a bookkeeping service bureau, or an accounting machine, or maybe he just needs a better accountant. If your firm sells computers, it is immediately incumbent upon you to determine whether your computer really *is* the way to solve his problem. If you think it might be, then your problem is to convince him that (a) he needs a computer, and (b) he needs *your* computer. In other words, you have three distinct chances to lose the sale. *But note:* The customer's *need* is for a solution. He may have some preconception of the way to solve it; however, if you honestly disagree with him, it is best to state your belief because if you sell him something that is mismatched in cost and capability to his actual needs, he will not be grateful.

During the course of introducing your product and analyzing customer needs, you may detect a substantial misfit. You may be selling a high-performance unit for $5,000, when in fact the market keeps asking for a minimal unit in the $2,000 range. You may have developed a technically advanced electronic actuator, when most needs could be satisfied by an inexpensive pneumatic unit. Or perhaps you're marketing a nicely packaged laboratory instrument that, if stripped, could be sold on volume OEM basis to builders of larger laboratory systems. The point is that, regardless of how hard you tried to analyze the market before starting your sales effort, your analysis is probably, in the heat of battle, going to prove wrong in some respects. One of the great strengths of small companies is their ability to adapt and change direction quickly; don't permit yourself to get locked into a losing situation by your business plan. The feedback from customers should be the principal consideration.

In analyzing the specific needs of prospective customers, try to remain sensitive also to their *other* needs as well. In selling chart recorders, for example, you may discover that there is a great need for chart paper that will not curl when humidity rises. This might be profitable additional business opportunity for your firm, if a suitable paper can be found and marketed through your organization. What else does this customer buy, anyway? If he buys typewriters, can you also offer him adding machines? Desks? Dictating equipment? If he buys machine tools, can you also sell him cutters? Measuring machines? Gages? If he buys pressure transducers, can you sell him a complete system with electronics? Your main cost in business for a long time is going to be that of reaching living, breathing customers. Make it your challenge to see how many of the needs of each one your firm can reasonably attempt to fill. Try not to freeze the definition of your business too early; the longer you can remain opportunistic, the better the chances you may uncover a much better opportunity than the one you set out to pursue.

SERVICING THE RELATIONSHIP

A major customer, even a tough one, is a priceless asset. However, it is surprising how many entrepreneurs are prone to ignore their existing customers in the thrill of the chase after new ones. Yet, logically, the emphasis should be reversed. The existing customer requires much less effort and cost to sell additional volume; if you do a good job with him, he will become your staunch advocate, enabling you to sell other firms more easily. He will provide the cash flow upon which your further marketing will be based. Therefore, be sure that you have exhausted every opportunity to satisfy him before turning your energies to the chase. This may mean:

1 / Occasional personal contact, just to make sure everything's OK (and to find out what the competition is saying to him, what he thinks of your salesman and of your product).

2 / Rapid field service when required. Follow-up procedures should be instituted to make sure the problem was actually solved. Don't take your technician's word for this.

3 / Personal involvement in any negotiations involving substantial purchase quantities or deviation from normal specifications.

4 / Occasional surveillance of the accounts receivable to make sure that petty items, such as spare parts or service bill-backs, are not creating irritation with the customer. Be prepared to bend (conspicuously) on these small matters.

5 / Little remembrances. While Christmas gifts, etc., are normally considered to be in poor taste, and are actively discouraged by most major firms, there are exceptional circumstances. If you feel that a particular customer relationship would be enhanced by a gift in good taste, and no rules dictate otherwise, it is probably OK. Occasional entertainment for the customer may be better, however, since it creates an atmosphere of personal rapport without the possible undesirable nuances of a gift.

As a final note on the value of customer relationships, try asking yourself the following:

---

1 / *How much have we invested in direct negotiations, man-hours, phone bills, travel, face-to-face contact with this customer?*

2 / *How many prospects did we have to sift before finding him? What did that cost us?*

3 / *How much did we spend in advertising, promotion, and prospecting before we even came up with that list of prospects?*

If most firms performed this calculation honestly, they would be astounded at the amount of actual hard dollars they have invested in each customer relationship. Be sure that each relationship is secure and fully exploited before rushing forth to invest in further ones.

HANDLING PROBLEMS

No matter how hard you try, sooner or later you're going to foul up. When it comes, it may be a real beauty. Picture this: You are two months late in delivering a machine to your customer. You've heard three times this week from his attorneys, but at last it's gone out the door. Next, the truck gets re-routed to Los Angeles instead of Minneapolis. Two weeks and several pints of blood later, the unit is delivered. Then you get a call at midnight from their president, informing you that the unit delivered was metric, and they ordered English.

What do you do now? Well, the first thing to do is face the fact that *you*—not your regional manager, your chief engineer, or your sales manager—had better handle this. When everything goes haywire, the customer expects to hear from the president—not from a hired hand. Trying to delegate at this point will make things worse. Depending upon the value of the customer and the possibility of some retaliatory action on his part, you may be well advised to propose a meeting at his plant, as opposed to trying to solve the problem over the phone. This has two advantages:

1 / Offering to get on a plane the next morning underscores the great concern on the part of your company. It reveals how *extraordinary* this circumstance is (never reveal that it also happened last week to somebody else).

2 / The time it takes for the meeting to occur gives everybody a chance to cool down and consider realistic solutions.

At this point, your skill as a negotiator will be put to the test. You must be willing to appear ready to make the situation right, even at the sacrifice of your firm. This proferred sacrifice may take the form of unbilled overtime to correct the problem; compensation for direct loss suffered by the customer; replacement or substitution of a loaner unit while his is being corrected; offering other compensatory considerations, such as extended payment terms, discounts, etc.

At this point, in reading the fine print on the back of your quotation form, you may discover some loophole or other that may seem to absolve you of liability for costs resulting from this problem. *Invoke the fine print at your peril.* If the customer feels that he has been slickered, you can forget about ever selling him anything again. Your safest tactic at this point is to ask the customer what *he* thinks is fair. This, in effect, places the burden of fairness upon him, and his demands may turn out to be unexpectedly reasonable.

In resolving problems of this sort, it is necessary to take the long view of the short-run concessions you may be considering. What did it cost us in dollars, energy, and calendar time to get this customer? What will it cost us to replace him? What will be the volume and profitability of sales with him over the next couple of years if we keep him? You may be much better off to relinquish the profit on this particular sale (or to take a loss) than to lose the customer. This negotiation is also a good opportunity to further solidify the loyalty of your customer by your manifest integrity and desire to make the situation right.

THE PROBLEM CUSTOMER

Every company eventually acquires a few problem customers. It is often difficult to balance the benefits of their business against the time, aggravation, and petty costs of doing business with them. These customers may fall into the following classes:

1 / *The slow payer.* Slow payment may be his business policy and will likely be justified by a sequence of "lost" invoices, product "deficiencies", etc. He may tell you that, prior to the sale, he told *your* salesman that he would pay when his customer pays *him.*

2 / *The specs changer.* This customer either feels that his needs are so unique that he *must* have a special version of your product (at the price of the standard unit), or he feels that, until delivery, he has the right to keep on making changes in the specifications at no cost.

3 / *The backroom lawyer.* This is the fellow who may have taken a commercial law course somewhere along the line and misses no opportunity to show his skill in outflanking his suppliers. He will find loopholes in your contract justifying eternal free service, exclusivity with his firm, product return privileges, and God knows what else.

4 / *The wheeler-dealer.* This is the customer who lets you know, none too subtly, that he's found another supplier willing to supply the same product as you for about 60 percent of your price. He will change suppliers for such marginal advantages that they are negated by the changeover costs, but he prides himself on being a tough negotiator. Anyway, his boss only hears about the savings he's made—not the costs of obtaining them.

These and other problem customers can absorb a very large portion of your time and energy in maintaining their business and heading off additional problems. When such a customer has identified himself, weigh realistically the benefits and costs of keeping him—then, if you must cut him off, have no compunctions. It is simply impossible to work with certain types of firms, and your decision connotes no failure on your part.

It is especially easy for new firms to acquire problem customers for several reasons. For example:

1 / The customer may have already been rejected by all the existing suppliers in the industry, and he comes to you as a new victim.

2 / The new firm often has inadequate or nonexistent credit check procedures or other sources of market intelligence.

3 / The salesman for the new firm will exert great pressure or temptation to take on what is perhaps a visibly marginal account.

4 / The new venture may seem like a softer touch to the problem customer than his bigger, older suppliers. When the heat is on, he will pay them first and let you wait.

The entrepreneur who intends to survive should be aware of these perils and be sure that some mechanism exists for a suitable degree of screening of new prospective customers. It's much better for all concerned to request payment in advance "until credit is established", even at the risk of affronting a customer, than to spend the next two years trying to collect.

ENFORCING CONTRACTS

It often develops that a business contract undertaken in good faith by buyer and seller becomes inappropriate to the emerging situation. For example, a customer may contract to purchase 1,000 of your units, and then discover that he can only use 200; completing the contract may be very poor business for him—in fact, it may put him out of business. Another firm may buy your equipment, only to discover that the job intended cannot be done on your equipment—despite the fact that the specifications of your equipment were clearly stated in your quotation, and regardless of the fact that you do not warrant "fitness for purpose".

You have a contract. The question is, To what extent do you enforce it? This is a business decision, not a legal one. If you succeed in pushing your contractual demands down the customer's throat, he is no longer a customer. In fact, he may become a very costly adversary in a courtroom. In selecting a route of action, you must again take the long view: What was the cost to obtain this customer? What is his future value to us? What will be the cost of enforcing our contract? What will be the *net* dollar gain on this contract from so doing? Will our willingness to negotiate simply be interpreted as softness, encouraging future transgressions? These are hard questions, but they should be asked *before* calling in the lawyers. A court action usually benefits nobody; it is, rather, evidence of failure and ineptitude on the part of both parties in solving their mutual problems to their better advantage. Above all, try to avoid involving your ego and emotions in a situation where, objectively speaking, you've been had. So doing merely diminishes the possibility of achieving any sort of rational decision and robs your energies from more creative enterprises.

| *CONVENTIONAL WISDOM* ⇦ ➡ **REALITY** |

You can delegate responsibility for customer relations to your marketing department while you attend to more important matters.	**You isolate yourself from your customer and his problems at your peril. You don't *have* anything more important to do.**

20

competitors
and
what
to do
about them

He that wrestles with us strengthens our nerves and sharpens our skill. Our antagonist is our helper.

✻ EDMUND BURKE ✻

WHO IS A COMPETITOR?

Your very earliest efforts to assess the market for your proposed product included an initial look at the competition. Once you are in business, however, it will become apparent that your initial definition of competitor may have been rather narrow. Most entrepreneurs tend to think of the competitor as the firm that has very nearly the same product for the same markets as his own. However, some reflection will reveal that the term *competition* is in fact much harder to define.

Conceptually, the competition is any other entity that is competing for the same funds that we are competing for. This means that the cinema operator is not just competing with other cinemas in his area; he is competing with all other entertainment media (e.g., sporting events, stage shows). The builder of hydraulic motors is not just in competition with other hydraulic motor firms—he is in competition with electric and pneumatic motor firms too. The vendor of consulting services is in competition not only with other consultants but also with in-house experts within the client's firm. In determining *what* sales appeal will be most successful, you must first place yourself in your customer's shoes and imagine what his real alternatives are. Then, and only then, can you compile a convincing case, contrasting your solution to the others.

COMPETITORS AS AN IDEA SOURCE

Enlightened imitation is among the surest roads to business success. It is beneath the dignity of no businessman to imitate, adapt, and improve upon the innovations of other companies. The incredible trajectory of the Japanese economy has been, until very recently, the result of intelligent adaption and improvement of nonoriginal ideas. On the other hand, England, long a pioneer in the inventive technologies, has been far less successful in innovation and adaption of existing ideas for commercial uses. The enormous advantage that the imitator has over the innovator is that the imitator does not have the development costs, the market testing, the unsuccessful false starts, and the tremendous lead times that plague the true innovator. Remember, the pioneer is the guy who gets an arrow in his back.

None of which is to say that your imitation must be blatant or unimaginative. Skillful adaption implies learning from the mistakes as well as the successes of the innovator. Very often, the second, third, or fourth imitator is the one who really rings the commercial bell through benefit of observing the mistakes and weaknesses of several other competitors. After all, IBM did not invent the computer, nor were they the first to market it. Moreover, they did not introduce xerography, although their entry into office copying incorporated a number of improvements.

It is also constructive to observe (where possible) some of the failures as well as the successes of your competitors. What products have they introduced with fanfare, but silently deleted from their last catalog? We all have our little Edsel, after all. Just be sure that your fantastic new design is not already *somebody else's* Edsel.

COMPETITORS AS A BASIS
FOR COMPARISON

In addition to such obvious comparisons as price, specifications, and share-of-market, some other comparisons may prove instructive to the extent they can be made. These include:

1 / Gross margins.

2 / Overall profitability.

3 / Allocation of sales dollars to labor, material, R & D, advertising, etc.

4 / Marketing set-up, salesman incentives, dealer policy.

5 / Areas of product development.

6 / Current market research in progress.

7 / Quantity and costs of materials purchases.

8 / Current production and shipping rates.

9 / Identity of major customers.

10 / Pricing policies, formulas.

Depending upon your situation, there may be a number of other things you ought to know about your competitor as well. This knowledge is almost essential for intelligent development of offensive strategy and defensive tactics. It is especially critical for the new enterprise because:

1 / New ventures are very often established because of a market gap, an oversight, or a quirk in the competitive structure. If this is about to change without your knowledge, the game may already be over.

2 / The established company, including competitors, can afford a few mistakes; one major mistake will probably kill the new venture. The easiest way to make it is by misreading the competition, both as to its plans and as to its probable reaction to your own planned actions.

FINDING OUT ABOUT COMPETITORS

Short of calling in the CIA, there are ways in which one can learn as much as necessary about competitors. The following list is only suggestive; the imaginative entrepreneur will be able to come up with others as the occasion demands.

1 / *Financial sources.* In addition to annual and interim reports, public companies must file various other classes of financial data and other information with government bodies. These include NYSE listing applications, SEC Form 10-K, offering circulars for new security issues, and, in some states, annual statements of condition. In addition, you can obtain Dun & Bradstreet or NCO reports. You can check with city hall to find out whether financing statements have been filed pledging collateral. You may also be able to unearth a financial analyst who has recently studied the company and can give you some insights without disclosing sensitive information.

2 / *Former employees.* One can often learn a good deal about a firm from its former employees—especially disgruntled ones. Even present employees are often a good source of intelligence when, for example, they are interviewed in response to a job opening you have advertised.

3 / *Dealers, reps, distributors.* These people are usually anxious to fill a sympathetic ear with their grievances against your competitor, whom they represent. You will learn about late deliveries, quality problems, design deficiencies, late commissions (cash problems), and field service problems to a degree that may astound you. Everybody has problems—even your smooth-looking competitor.

4 / *Suppliers.* A classical example occurred a few years ago, wherein a firm making motors had always carefully guarded its volume data. Its competitor, however, discovered the source for one of the key purchased components in the motors, which *in turn* had one key purchased component. The level 2 vendor unconsciously gave away the monthly shipping volume of his customer's customer without ever having heard of the motor manufacturer. There are several ways to approach your competitor's supplier. The best way is as a potential customer. You'd like to see the shop; you'd like to see what sort of work he's doing for others in the industry; you'd like to get some idea of how much he could ship you when volume is required. In short, give him as many opportunities as you can to tell you what a great job he's doing for your competitor.

5 / *Professional meetings.* Pay attention to what the competitor's scientist is saying about his work. His president might be quite chargrined at the amount of competitive information being disclosed in the interest of scientific progress. Observe also what they are writing in the professional journals.

6 / *Other companies' salesmen.* While competitor A's salesman will probably be quite close-mouthed about his company's activities, he may be quite effusive (and knowledgeable) about the activities of your mutual competitor B. What-are-those-people-up-to-now is a favorite game played in hotel bars across the nation every night. Likewise, the salesmen for their suppliers can be a source of some occasional insight.

7 / *Unethical sources.* While there is in reality a continuum of "ethicalness" from pure white to pure black, most of us think we know about where the line is. Methods such as espionage techniques, bribery, employee "plants", etc., are not unknown in business. Ethical questions aside, however, such questionable methods seldom justify the cost of possible exposure and are likely to backfire. Once your own integrity is called into question, there is no real way to repair the damage.

COMPETITIVE STRUCTURE

There are, roughly speaking, three distinct types of competitive structures:

Type A: The market dominated by one large competitor. IBM is the classic example in the computer industry.

Type B: The market shared by five to twenty fairly comparable firms. The semiconductor industry might be cited as an example.

Type C: The fragmented market, shared by dozens of small competitors. Film processing is an industry of this type.

In picking new markets for your firm, you are probably better off with either Type A or Type C competition than Type B. In Type A, you will not be as likely to encounter immediate retaliatory action, and your pricing may be supported under the large company's pricing umbrella. Granted, you may be very weak when at last he retaliates in some way, but usually you can find some job he isn't doing too well and prosper at filling the gap. Also, he risks antitrust action in moving to limit your competition.

A Type C market permits a vigorous firm to establish market dominance rather quickly by outselling or buying out the small competitors. If you can become the dominant force in this market, then *you* will be establishing the pricing, the standards, and the rate-of-change for the industry.

Type B markets, in contrast to the others, are tough to enter because they have strong incentive to retaliate quickly to additional competitive pressures; because market dominance will be difficult, if not impossible, to achieve; and because existing competition among co-equals probably has eliminated any comfortable price umbrella, allowing you no temporary period of extraordinary profits to offset start-up costs.

HIRING COMPETITORS' PERSONNEL

The hiring of competitors' personnel is as much a part of the American competitive tradition as the spitball. The rate of success of new ventures, it could be argued, would be greatly diminished were it not for the ready availability of experienced (i.e., competitors') personnel. One of the reasons, in fact, why it is much easier to start a company in the United States than in many other countries is the lack of any excessive employee loyalty and the general absence of ethical sanctions against job-hoppers. In the United States, the job is considered to be something you do until something better comes along. In more traditional societies, such as Japan and Germany, on the other hand, your employer is a sort of alter-father to whom you owe loyalty, in return for security.

Often, there is simply no alternative to hiring competitors' personnel. If there is a scarcity of skills, you and your local competitor are almost automatically bidding up the price for those skills. However, even in cases where there *is* a choice, many firms believe they are better off to hire the competitor's employee, rather than recruiting from outside the industry. The reasons are pretty obvious:

1 / They help themselves *and* handicap the competitor in a single act.

2 / The employee likely will require minimal training and break-in time since he already knows your business.

3 / They may be able to elicit important information from him regarding the competitor's operations and customers.

However, the advantages can be short-lived since two can play the game. Moreover, the job-hopper doesn't become a loyal company man just because he comes to work for you; he may be working for another competitor (or maybe the original one) in another year with *your* business plan in his file.

Economists have argued that, on the whole, job-hopping may benefit the economy by promoting competition; information flows so freely between companies that nobody can keep a secret for very long. This is slight comfort to the entrepreneur interested in survival, however. Perfect competition is exactly what he *doesn't* need. Employee swapping, like price cutting, is one of those things most businessmen would like to see go away; however, until human nature changes significantly, it is with us to stay. The pragmatic entrepreneur must resign himself to playing the game, initially at least, by whatever rules his particular industry dictates.

PART V

RUNNING

THE

SHOW

21

a
race
with
the
clock

Show me a good loser and I'll show you a loser.

* ANONYMOUS *

The day that your Round One financing is complete, the document signed, and the cash in the bank is the day you begin a contest—perhaps the toughest of your life. It is a race with the clock or, more accurately, with the calendar. You have succeeded in convincing investors of the merit of your deal. They have delivered. Now it's your turn. In your business plan you yourself wrote the rules and time limits in which the game was to be played. Those dates that once seemed like soft targets to you now take on the character of grim deadlines. Your cash-flow projections tell you when you will run out of cash; whether you can get more at that point depends upon how well you've met your other objectives. If you go through the money and the results aren't visible, it doesn't matter whose fault it is— the game is over.

THE IMPORTANCE OF MEETING TARGETS

In the early phases of operations it is very often tempting to move the targets around, rather than making a genuine effort to hit them. It is nearly always true, for example, that engineers will want a couple of more months to polish the product design before it is released for production. Or maybe now that you've got money in the bank, this is the time to find some nicer quarters, instead of putting the money and energy into the marketing set-up as planned. Nothing is more upsetting to the initial operations of the company than an immediate abandonment of the plan.

241

Needless to add, this makes your investors not a little uncomfortable as well. Get into the habit of holding your own dates as earnestly as you hold your customer delivery dates. Get into the habit of meeting targets.

ENTREPRENEURS VERSUS CUSTODIANS

Very early in the game of operating a new company, you may come to recognize that your own activities fall more or less into two categories: the entrepreneurial and the custodial. Roughly defined, the entrepreneurial tasks involve the *setting up, planning,* and *motivational* activities of the firm. They would include such things as initiating market research; recruiting a banker, an accountant, an ad agency; finding a building; setting budgets; and so on. The custodial tasks, by contrast, are such things as tracking budgets, developing financial reports, purchasing materials, supervising production, refereeing disputes between production and marketing. Entrepreneurial tasks are much less delegable as a rule than are custodial tasks.

Also, among managers there is a spectrum ranging from pure entrepreneur to pure custodian, along which everyone falls. Although you will be obliged for some period to handle *both* the entrepreneurial and custodial tasks of your company, it is well to decide, based on your perception of yourself in the spectrum, which tasks you should get rid of by delegation and which you should keep to yourself. You might be successful at delegating certain entrepreneurial tasks (e.g., advertising responsibility) while hanging on to certain custodial tasks where you feel a strong interest (e.g., accounts receivable management). Yet, in general the more of the custodial tasks you can get rid of without losing control, the better job you're probably going to do as an entrepreneur. However, as the company matures and its operations require skilled custodians, you may find that you must move aside or move out. It is generally recognized that entrepreneurs often make lousy managers.

THE PRINCIPLE OF ENLIGHTENED MEDIOCRITY

The author is indebted to Nick De Wolf, founder of Teradyne Corporation, for this pungent phrase, which captures so beautifully the essence of what every successful entrepreneur learns sooner or later. Basically, it is this: There is very little hope for a perfectionist trying to run a growing new enterprise. There are *so* many things to be done, *so* many problems to solve that weren't in the business plan, and *so* little time to do it in that a first-rate job is not just impossible for each—it may be undesirable. It has been asserted, with some truth, that we accomplish about 80 percent of any given project with the first 20 percent of the effort— which says, mathematically at least, that one should be able to do about five 80 percent quality jobs with the time and energy required to do a *single* 100 percent A+ on any of them. The entrepreneur who shoots for 80 percent quality will not go far wrong. There are, nevertheless, some areas that you will wish to single out for 100 percent quality treatment. It may be product quality control, customer service, or some one or two other key areas that drastically affect the company's position in the marketplace. In these areas, you must ruthlessly demand perfection; in the others, you should learn to settle for less without getting ulcers. To illustrate a bit further, a certain sort of manager may spend a month working out the details of a computerized production control system for the shop when, in fact, about the same result might be obtained with a couple of wall charts in the foreman's office. In fact, the result may be better if the foreman thought of it himself. In learning to settle for 80 percent in most areas, you at least have a fighting chance in your race with the clock.

CASH BALANCE

Among the hardest things for the starting enterpreneur to get onto is the function of cash in the enterprise. It seems incredible to many that a company with growing sales and good profits could go bankrupt, but it happens. It happens because the very condition of growth can create overextension of existing working capital and cash. When and if the company's bank debt is called and cannot be renewed (as in the cash crunch of 1970), good companies as well as bad go down the tube. A major customer's failure, a serious collection problem, or a supplier problem can have the same effect.

The existence of a good-sized lump of cash in the bank following financing tends to distract attention from the crucial significance of the cash balance as the company's blood supply. Then, one cold morning, it is gone; it has been devoured by the business operations: equipment, materials, salaries, work-in-process, development. At this point it dawns on many managers for the first time what that cash-flow projection really is: a survival weapon.

A manager who cannot predict a cash shortage in his business is not running the company—the company is running *him*. An unexpected cash crisis can cause much embarrassment and in some cases permanent damage (e.g., bankruptcy) to the company. It may make it impossible to meet such "no-fall" commitments as loan interest, the payroll, or (God forbid) withholding tax payment. To say that this event reduces the confidence of the bank, the staff, or the government is to somewhat understate the case. It is damned serious. Other forms of awkwardness can include missed shipping dates due to materials withheld by suppliers; panic calls to your investors from suppliers; emergency calls to one's investors to help meet the Friday payroll; major price concessions to customers to obtain early payment. Not so nice.

The best and only way to avoid this is to *plan* your cash flow, and guard it jealously. Work out a format appropriate to *your* needs with your accountant. Schedule your accounts receivable into it *by major customer* so that you can pinpoint collection problems one by one. Schedule major cash payments *by major supplier* or so that aggregation does not hide reality. Try to plan about six months ahead; review and update weekly. If you see a cash shortage developing two months out, *now* is the time to do something about it. Go see your banker, go over your cash-flow statement with him, show him when and why the shortage will develop, plus when and how the desired loan will be liquidated. He will be far more disposed to cooperate now than 60 days hence when your checks unexpectedly start bouncing. So even if there is no cash shortage now, start operating as though there were. Sooner or later there will be. You may be growing faster than expected, or another cash crunch may cause your customers to start delaying payment, or something may go wrong with a major shipment causing delayed payment. Get control of your cash today. Your race with the clock can be equated with a race to reverse the direction of the flow from negative to positive before crossing zero—not unlike pulling an aircraft out of a dive.

MAINTAINING INVESTOR RAPPORT

You can make no greater mistake than shutting your investors off from the progress of the company or, worse, permitting an attitude of suspicion or hostility to develop between you. One of the functions of directors' meetings is, theoretically, to keep the investors informed. Unless the investors insist on them, however, most entrepreneurs can find better things to do with their time than holding a directors' meeting. This, however, in no way absolves you of the need to keep your investors informed. A monthly memorandum to the investors detailing large pending orders, various nonfinancial milestones attained, significant research results, developments in the marketplace, etc., will be very valuable. Attach recent press clippings, literature, etc. Its functions include:

1 / Offsetting the impact of the (probably bad) news in the monthly financial statements.

2 / Giving them some interesting information on their deal.

3 / Letting them know you care what they think, creating vicarious participation.

4 / Establishing a fund of goodwill upon which you can draw when the company is in a cash crisis, or when you are raising large amounts of additional capital and require their votes for approval.

The stockholder who is ignored until there is a problem, or until his vote is needed for some deal that has sprung on the scene, is going to be understandably difficult to deal with. Make the effort to keep him on your side as a partner in the venture.

THE ENTREPRENEUR'S CREDIBILITY

As noted earlier, the importance of hitting your early targets can't be overemphasized. This is the honeymoon with investors, with suppliers, with the bank, with customers. Your performance will never again be under such intense scrutiny because they are all still nervous about you, your integrity, your ability to perform.

If all goes along nicely and according to schedule, you have nothing to worry about. Just be sure they all know what a lot of effort it took to do it. If, however, things do not go exactly right, your credibility can still be salvaged. When serious problems arise, you will be very foolish indeed to try to hide them to make yourself look good. Most business problems get worse with time (e.g., quality problems, collections problems, employee dishonesty), and by the time you *have* to acknowledge them, the situation can be very bad indeed. You can have problems *and* investor support if you acknowledge the problem and, if meaningful, ask for help.

Naturally, the same principle applies to your customers and suppliers as well. If you discover that a shipping deadline is going to be blown, it is far better that the customer learn about it immediately from the president than from your shipper on the scheduled delivery day. If you're going to be late in paying a large invoice, have the courage to call your supplier personally and explain; give him a chance to plan *his* cash requirements around your problem. Tell him when you *will* pay and make it happen. These may all seem to be rather obvious, common-sense actions, but when things get rough you're going to need these people. If they doubt your integrity, they won't be there.

PLANNING YOUR TIME

Most entrepreneurs do a much better job at planning the year's activities for the entire company than they do planning their own day. Consequently, they end up taking 14 hours to accomplish what should be done in 10 (hence, including Saturdays, the legendary 84-hour work week). However, despite a certain heroic aura borne by the 84-hour week, it is really dsyfunctional and can almost always be shown to be due to poor planning, rather than heroic devotion. It is dysfunctional for the company because:

1 / After about 10 hours of work, anybody's efficiency tapers off enormously; you will accomplish little more during the next four hours than you would in one hour fresh.

2 / It creates an atmosphere of tacit disapproval toward other employees who can't or won't work your hours. This can strain the relations between you and key people.

3 / The long hours are naturally necessary when the big push is on. As a steady diet, however, they merely exhaust you and rob you of the vitality necessary to get customers

excited about your product, or to inspire your own employees.

The better answer is to try planning your day better. A few tips:

===

1 / Identify your own "creativity cycle" during the day, and be sure that those hours are reserved for your really creative work.

2 / Try scheduling your entire day—not just appointments— scheduling yourself as though you were an expensive production machine (you are). Have *specific* attainable goals or milestones to be accomplished in each interval of time.

3 / Ignore the telephone. Save one hour at the less creative part of your day to return all calls. Do not become the slave of this instrument. Use your secretary to filter off (politely) all but the most vital callers.

4 / Work outside the office. If you have a major report, 5-year plan, technical paper, or speech to prepare, go work someplace else (not at home). A library is often the best place to get things done.

5 / Try batching, rather than real-time operation. Set up a few regular weekly, bi-weekly, or monthly meetings to keep abreast of progress in specific areas, rather than constantly interrupting your employees' work or letting them interrupt yours.

6 / Batch your travel. This is often less costly in out-of-pocket terms, as well as being efficient. If you plan to be gone two solid weeks next March, everyone knows you'll be away and can plan around you.

7 / Batch your correspondence. Get used to using a dictating machine instead of dictating to your secretary (you'll get a better employee for the same money if you don't require shorthand), so you don't keep interrupting her work. Batching your correspondence permits you to get all files, orders, etc., in order and get it all done quickly.

8 / Use the telex instead of commiting yourself to long telephone conversations. It is cheaper, just as fast, and gives a written record. Try using it also instead of writing letters. People will forgive you if you're terse. Remember, the average business letter costs over $6.00 to dictate, type, and send.

9 / Set aside some time for thinking—even if it's only a half-hour in the shower each morning. Nothing is more inimical to good management than a constant rat-race with every minute jammed full.

10 / Don't overdo priorities. Some things are important—others are merely urgent in a time sense. Some require large blocks of uninterrupted concentration while others are short and can be fitted into the time interstices between more important or nonschedulable events. Don't get yourself tied up in a system that tackles everything in order of "importance" or "priority".

11 / Get some regular exercise. There is no better defense against the physical and emotional depreciation of the entrepreneur than some daily energetic exercise. It helps you wake up, digest your food better, and maintain a higher general level of animal vitality.

12 / Get out of the office. Whether to work on a major project, or have lunch with your banker, or make some sales calls with the local rep, make it a point to get out of the office and frequently expose yourself to new people and fresh ideas. This helps to revitalize both you and your staff.

13 / Employ the principle of enlightened procrastination. It is truly amazing the number of problems that, if ignored, simply disappear. Someone else solves them, or a deadline passes, or the need for their performance disappears, or somebody discovers it really wasn't needed after all. In sorting out your "In" box, you will discover that about 70 percent of its contents can be put in the circular file, 20 percent in a bushel box marker "pending," and the 10 percent remainder earmarked for action sometime this week.

REFERENCES

1 / Webber, Ross A., *Time and Management.* New York: Van Nostrand Reinhold Co., 1972.

A 160-page essay on time, how it gets lost, and concrete measures for its management as a corporate resource. This book, although intended for the manager of the established firm, has many important insights for the entrepreneur.

22

more
on
negotiation

Let us never negotiate out of fear, but let us never fear to negotiate.

* John F. Kennedy *

Many successful business executives would, if pressed, acknowledge that negotiating skill, more than specific business knowledge, administrative technique, or other management skills, has influenced their ability to achieve. Negotiation is the common, central element in *all* of business—whether between two camel traders in the bazaar or between General Motors and a tough labor union. Skill in negotiation appears to be one constant factor in nearly any successful enterprise. It is extraordinary, therefore, that it is seldom if ever treated explicitly in business schools or other management development programs.

Negotiation impinges on nearly every activity in business life, regardless of the size of the enterprise. It is especially significant, however, in the early operations of a new company. An established firm has the substance, the ongoing sales, the reputation for delivery and payment, and a huge vested interest to project. They have much to offer as well as to gain from their opposing negotiators. Contrast this, then, to the situation of the new company: It has no record, no significant substance, no proven ability to deliver on its promises; worse yet, the opposing negotiator may have had some unfavorable experience with very small companies. Nonetheless, the only way that substance, track record, and reputation *can* be built by the new firm is through negotiation.

You will at the outset be negotiating lines of credit with suppliers and banks; compensation packages with employees and prospective employees; complex, multi-dimensional contracts with customers. You may find yourself also negotiating with people who are supposed to be your paid helpers. For example, you may become engaged in a negotiation with your auditor over proper treatment of inventories.

YOUR OPPONENT IS USUALLY AT
A GROSS ADVANTAGE

In Chapter 12, we observed that the financier with whom you are negotiating for capital is invariably at a great advantage over you, the entrepreneur. This is also true to some significant degree of nearly every
other outside entity with whom you may be negotiating in the early stages
of growth. Your opposer is negotiating similar deals with other companies
every day of the year. He has heard all your arguments before and knows
how to counter them; he has seen three better deals than yours already
this week; moreover, he probably understands the strengths and weaknesses of your position better than you do yourself. Finally, he probably
needs your patronage a great deal less than you need his—and he knows it.

In short, the entrepreneur is attempting to negotiate a place in the
world for his company at the very time when his inexperience, coupled
with the firm's lack of substance, least qualify him for success. Therefore,
he should take whatever steps are possible toward improving the probable
outcome by:

1 / Improving his own negotiating skills, and

2 / Enlisting the skills of experienced negotiators.

THE NEGOTIATING PROCESS [1]

Inexperienced negotiators are often handicapped by their very concept
of what a negotiation is supposed to be. They tend to view the process
as a form of combat in which there will be a winner and a loser; tactics
and strategies will be used, if at all, to drive the other guy to the wall.
To back this up, logically, they would tend to believe that the threat of
force (play it my way or else) will elicit the desired concessions from
one's opposer.

---

[1] The author is much indebted to Gerard I. Nierenberg for several of the
key ideas in this section (see "References").

A little reflection will reveal how invalid this view of negotiation actually is. First, there would be no negotiation at all if both parties did not perceive some potential benefit from it. In fact, the purpose of negotiation is precisely to establish how the *joint* benefits of a new situation can be made to exceed the benefits of the old situation. To put it in economists' terms, you both should be striving toward a *higher* tradeoff curve—not merely forcing one another up and down the same curve you both started from. Second, it is an experience of everyday life that "agreements" struck under duress tend only to last until the weaker party feels he has the strength to tear them up. If your opposing party *feels* he has been driven to the wall (whether or not it really *is* a bad deal for him), his prime energies from that point forward will be directed toward evening the score with you. The fact that he may be violating a contract to accomplish this merely ensures that your lawyer will be kept busy in the future.

A second handicap with which inexperienced people enter a negotiating session is that of a prematurely frozen position (here's our deal, take it or leave it). There is almost no way you could better guarantee that you will not get *anything* you want from a negotiation than by presenting an ultimatum demanding everything. Even if you feel that what you desire is reasonable, attainable, and beneficial to some degree to the opposing party, you must *still* let him prove all this to himself. He must take the intervening steps himself. Along the way it is possible that he will come up with alternative formulations that you haven't even considered that may be more beneficial for both parties (e.g., a method of structuring the purchase of a company to minimize the taxes for both sides).

KNOW YOUR OPPONENT

The better understanding you have of the individual you will be facing in a major negotiation, the better your chances will be of working successfully with him. Some basic facts on his education, business background, tax status, and general personality can be truly invaluable. What personal needs is he going to satisfy by entering this negotiation? Sometimes it is difficult to find out much in advance along these lines, especially if the organization with which you are negotiating elects to put in a new man to run the negotiation. However, rather than going at it cold, you may be able to use some tactic, such as a "fact-finding meeting" or other occasion to meet with the individual prior to the actual negotiation. You may also be able to identify someone who has recently dealt with the person in a similar context.

It is also desirable to know a good deal about the organization he represents. What are their unannounced motives? What are their legal constraints? How far have they gone with firms similar to yours? What is general practice in their industry? What special circumstances might cause them to bend their policies slightly in your case?

For a concrete example let us assume you are applying for a line of credit from a local bank. Their motivation for dealing with you may be a good deal more complex than simply a lender finding another borrower. They may have some *motivation* to deal with you because:

1 / Your firm is local, only a few blocks from their office.

2 / Your account, though small, has the possibility of growing very large.

3 / Your firm's presence will attract the private accounts of your employees to their bank.

4 / They may need to create an image of public servant, friend of small business, supporter of the prevailing minority in the neighborhood, etc.

However, on some investigation you may find that they have definite *limits* imposed by regulatory agencies and charter, such as:

1 / Requiring signature of the principal on unsecured notes.

2 / Balance sheet tests (e.g., debt–equity ratio).

3 / Avoiding long-term debt, as opposed to seasonal or self-liquidating loans.

4 / Charging higher rates for riskier loans.

In addition, they may have operating *policies* that, in times of tight cash, funnel money to their older customers instead of shaky new accounts. They may or may not prefer the pledging of assets (e.g., receivables). All of these are facts that, if known in advance, would greatly simplify the entrepreneur's negotiating process. It might, in fact, convince him that no negotiation was even warranted. The point is the more you can learn in advance about your opposer and his organization, the better.

STRATEGIES AND TACTICS

Negotiation is an art upon which substantial study has been expended, especially in the application area of labor relations. It is not the purpose of this book to advance the frontiers of this literature, but merely to catalog a few of the approaches that the entrepreneur may find useful and also that he should anticipate having used against him in negotiation. Nierenberg offers the following:

1 / *Forbearance.*   Hold off answering, call a recess, suspend discussions, call a "cooling off period". This will sometimes give the opposition a chance to see the merit of your position, to break the momentum of a negotiation that is going poorly, or just to show that *you* are under no time pressure to reach agreement.

2 / *Surprise.*   Often a skilled negotiator may elect to become totally unreasonable during a negotiation to take his opposer off balance. Surprise can also take the form of totally altered demands, a whole new set of facts injected, a relaxation of some "non-negotiable" demand, etc.

3 / *Fait accompli.*   Make your move; then let the other side react as they will. For example, if a final written contract is unsatisfactory, cross out those portions you dislike, initial each correction and sign the document. Or if there is disagreement on a price, simply write the check for the amount you think it should be and let *them* decide if the difference is worth the cost of collecting it.

4 / *Bland withdrawal.*   (Who, me?) Sometimes it's better to violate someone's presumed rights for a while than trying to negotiate initially. For example, you might elect to violate a known patent for a while to get established in a market, calculating either that it won't get enforced or that it will be worth your while to pay whatever the possible penalty would be.

5 / *Apparent withdrawal.* This can often be combined with surprise for the desired dramatic effect. Stomping indignantly out of a meeting can be risky but is used effectively by some negotiators. The threat of withdrawal can be equally effective if the demands of the opposer seem unrealistic.

6 / *Reversal.* In one form, this can mean the exacting of symmetric concessions from the opposing side. For example, if the union feels wages should go up because profits went up, oblige them to agree to wage cuts in case profits go down. In another form, reversal could cause you to increase your bargaining demands rather than lowering them in exchange for other concessions. For example, after a recess from financial negotiations in Boston, you could conspicuously "disappear" to New York for a few days, later reopening negotiations with a much higher price-per-share demand. Let your opposer wonder who you saw in New York.

7 / *Time limit.* The press of the calendar often provides the best impetus to a speedy conclusion. If your position will be served by time pressure, schedule your meeting a few days before Christmas or before the opposer's plant shutdown. Look how many negotiations are settled in Congress just before recess. Other limitations are useful as well. For example, in raising capital if your opposer knows your company will be out of cash shortly, he has a very real limit working in his favor.

8 / *Feinting.* Yield the concessions you make reluctantly. Make the opposition work for them. Bury the opposer in facts to conceal the weaknesses in your proposition. Make sure they know there is someone else very eager for a piece of your proposition. Let them feel at the end that they should be glad they got as good a deal as they did.

9 / *Participation.* Explain *why* the proposed package is unacceptable, and ask the opposer's help in showing how your problems with it can be answered. Enlist his ideas in a sincere, nonmanipulative way. This may result in a solution or in his recognition and acknowledgement that his position is unrealistic.

10 / *Dissociation.*   Make sure he understands why your firm is totally different from those other new ventures in which he lost all that money. Be sure your customer is able to differentiate between your product and all its scurrilous imitators.

11 / *Crossroads.*   Be prepared to meet any unreasonable new demand with an equally unreasonable counter-demand, until the initial demand is withdrawn. If labor wants a shorter workweek, you agree, provided they give up several paid holidays.

12 / *Blanketing.*   Inundate the opposer with data, with detailed questions, with prearranged meeting agendas, etc., to take away their initiative.

13 / *Randomizing.*   This can involve non-negotiating tactics, such as splitting the difference, flipping a coin, etc., all invoking irrational chance to break deadlocks.

14 / *Nonrandom Sample.*   As evidence, you introduce verbatim interview recordings with 10 engineers who like your product. Of course, you don't tell them about the other 50 who hate your stuff.

15 / *Salami.*   Try for small concessions, a slice at a time. Get them in the habit of saying yes. Tell the customer you only want to give him a sample of your product at an introductory price, etc. This is an especially common tactic in large corporations.

16 / *Shifting levels.*   If your opposer keeps pleading that he hasn't the authority to grant that concession, then go over his head. You may then be talking to a higher person with broader understanding as well as authority. Or make a supplier justify his price in terms of his costs instead of benefits to you. Or shift time horizons. Try negotiating for a whole year's supply, rather than simply for the next price-break quantity.

This list of negotiating tactics can be greatly expanded by your own experience, as you discover what works well for you.

SOME ADDITIONAL CONSIDERATIONS ON NEGOTIATING

Some advance preparation for any negotiation will serve you well. In addition to scouting the opposer fairly well, you should be sure that you have done your homework in other areas, too. Try to anticipate which way the negotiation will go, and be prepared with counter-tactics. Try to anticipate objections to your position and have the counter-arguments and facts available to back you up. Some people find play-acting simulation a useful preparation. Cite chapter and verse. Be prepared to justify all demands (even your arbitrary ones) in terms of rational considerations that the other side can accept. For example: "We cannot consider owning less than 52 percent of your stock because otherwise we cannot file a consolidated earnings statement with the IRS." Or; "I cannot meet your price demand because I would be in violation of the Sherman Anti-Trust Act." Let them know you would happily concede the point, if only you had a choice.

Try to maintain control of the place of the meeting as well as the agenda. The order, as well as the content, of the agenda can be very important—for example, if there is a time limit, reserve your weakest areas for last, so that they may get cut out altogether. Try to keep the initiative.

Be sure that you get an attorney who is a skilled and experienced negotiator, and that you have him present as a team member in any significant negotiation. There is no better protection against your own inexperience.

If there are others who must ratify the agreement reached by negotiation (e.g., key stockholders or partners) try to have them present at the negotiation, or at least keep them fully informed of progress so that they will know not only where you are but also how you got there. This will make it far easier to enlist their cooperation at the final stage. Try to remember that to succeed, the final agreement has to be good for everybody. If any principal feels he's being coerced or shortchanged, the agreement will probably be in litigation next year.

REFERENCES

1 / Nierenberg, G. I., *Creative Business Negotiating.* New York: Hawthorn Books, Inc., 1971.

2 / Nierenberg, G. I., *The Art of Negotiating.* New York: Cornerstone Library, 1971.

These two references are about the best books available on the area of negotiation. Both discuss Nierenberg's "needs theory".

3 / Strange, M., *Acquisition and Merger Negotiating Strategy.* New York: Hawthorne Books, Inc., 1971.

This is a very useful work on negotiating strategy, from the viewpoint of the acquiring firm. Required reading for those about to be acquired.

23

lawyers
and
their
uses

It's impossible to tell where what is legal ends and where justice begins.

A lawyer can do a good deal more for the businessman than advise him as to whether or not a proposed course of action is legal. That, in fact, is probably the least creative of the many services that the right lawyer can render. Besides being a legal advisor, he functions as a business advisor, a negotiator, an interface with the financial community, a soundingboard for ideas, and, of course, a defender, should the occasion demand. A top attorney, rather than being a mechanic, is an artist. He will be able to envision creative solutions to problems of organization, taxation, and finance that would probably never occur to you. He will also be able to look ahead and anticipate problems and take whatever measures are appropriate to minimize them. He can deploy a wide range of knowledge, experience, and contacts to help you to solve your problems.

LAWYERS AS LEGAL ADVISORS

In the mechanical aspects of incorporation, qualifying you to operate in various states, electing officers, directors, etc., you do not need the top man in the corporate law field. However, if, at the outset, there are serious questions regarding employment contracts with your previous employer, or questions of nondisclosure, noncompetition, or patent agreements, then you'd better have a pretty good man. The earlier in your corporate life you find your permanent attorney, the better the quality of important decisions you'll be making from now on will be.

Rather early on there will be questions as to the distribution of equity to employees, and you will need help and advice in drafting a stock purchase or stock option plan. There will be employment agreements, or at least invention disclosure agreements for your key people. There will be commercial terms and conditions to be worked out. At the appropriate stage, there will be the need for some legal assistance in the preparation of a business plan for the raising of seed and, later, Round One money. These are all activities in which legal and business advice blend to some extent, and you will want the best possible advice in their pursuit.

LAWYERS AS BUSINESS ADVISORS

In addition to the component of business advice inherent in the drafting of the contracts of the company, there are other areas in which it makes sense to enlist the ideas of your attorney. If his corporate law practice is an active one, he has come across many successful and not-so-successful businessmen and business ideas. This experience is at your disposal. He can be useful, for example, in suggesting tactics for collection of difficult accounts receivable; in proposing ways to deal with a partner who's gone sour; in dealing with the angry customer; in structuring stock offerings, purchase and sale agreements, etc., to take maximum advantage of tax laws. This list is only suggestive, but the point is that your attorney is in a position to have seen every conceivable sort of business problem, and is the best person to help you work around them or work out of them. Finally, be sure that you weigh your attorney's business advice, but make your own decisions. Attorneys are much better at identifying alternative courses of action and potential pitfalls than they are at evaluating the risks and probabilities. That's *your* job.

LAWYERS AS NEGOTIATORS

In a complex negotiation (e.g., a major contract with a customer, a stock underwriting agreement with an investment banker, or a sellout agreement with another firm), an attorney skilled in negotiation will probably save you many times his fee (which itself may be quite sizeable). The training and experience of attorneys in the adversary process, in the skilled researching of statute and precedent, and in the relativistic defense of the guilty as well as the innocent equip the attorney admirably to help you negotiate against other skilled negotiators. He can help you to sharpen up the objectives of the negotiation, to develop a negotiating strategy, and to help you counter the unexpected turn in discussions (see Chapter 23). In short, he can be a most formidable ally when you most need one.

LAWYERS AS INVESTOR INTERFACE

When you are raising funds for your venture, your lawyer is a most logical place to ask for suggestions as to possible investors. After all, he may have money himself and maybe a lot of affluent friends; moreover, he probably has some affluent clients, some of whom might be interested in exactly your kind of deal. He will, after having helped you draft your business plan or offering memorandum, have a double incentive to help you pull off the financing; he knows his chances of getting paid will be a whole lot better if you have money. And after having helped draft or review the document, he will have a detailed knowledge of your deal that will greatly help him in discussing it with other potential investors.

As a result of having handled private placements and public offerings in the past, your attorney should have some acquaintances in the investment banking community who can prove helpful. Finally, he may be helpful in identifying and introducing you to your future banker.

LAWYERS AS DEFENDERS

A hoary cliché has it, "When you're playing the game hard, you're going to get called offside once in a while." The penalty may come in the form of a lawsuit by an angry customer or employee; it may be an action brought against you by your stockholders; it may even be a petition for involuntary bankruptcy brought by panicked creditors. In any of the above, you're going to need a lot more from your attorney than friendly legal advice. You're going to need some decisive, intelligent action. This is where experience, skill, and prestige often hold the balance.

PICKING A LAWYER

In the selection of an attorney, unlike the selection of an auditor, the man is everything. He may be working in a large, prestigious firm or in a smaller firm, depending upon his inclinations. He may even work independently. There are those who believe that, other things being equal, you're better off with a good man in a big firm than a good man in a small firm. The arguments are (predictably):

1 / The large firm has a better-known name, which may in some circumstances be of value; at least it won't handicap you.

2 / The larger firm has a range of specialists in such matters as taxation, real estate, securities regulation, etc., who may from time to time be useful to you.

3 / The large firm has more people to draw from since your own lawyer may occasionally not be available.

In behalf of the small firm, you can probably expect more attention from the senior partners, you may find that people are more informal and accessible, and you may discover, too, that as an entrepreneur himself, your attorney has a generally better gut feel for your situation. It is the author's overall view that the new entrepreneur may be better off with the smaller firm in many cases. However, large versus small firm is not an issue of paramount importance. Selection of a good man is the key issue.

Your best source of leads for good lawyers is other entrepreneurs. Whom are they using? Whom have they dropped? What (if any) difficult situations have they confronted with this attorney and how did it go? What sorts of fees have they experienced? Did the man ask for stock or finder's fees in connection with financing (both considered mildly unethical)? Does the man seem to have plenty of good connections in the business and financial worlds? How has he been as an informal business advisor? How are his negotiating skills? These and other questions should be used to probe for actual information. Don't settle for an offhand, "Oh, our lawyer's a great guy—you'll really like him."

Recommendations from bankers, owners of large businesses, and other nonentrepreneurial types are likely to be slightly suspect because the recommender is suggesting somebody *he* would wish to have represent him—but his business problems are radically different from your own. As far as the local bar association is concerned, forget it. You might as well be looking in the Yellow Pages.

In interviewing the prospective lawyer, take along your first-cut business plan. Have a list of questions thought out ahead of time. Take up the same issues you raised with the other entrepreneurs. Who are some of his other corporate clients? Is there a present or downstream conflict? How much time is he going to be able to spend with you? With whom will you work when he's not available? How about fees? (Anywhere from $30 to $150 per hour may be justifiable). Will he take some collection cases on a contingency basis? (Probably he won't if he's a top man.) How about his experience in financing and in public offerings and SEC registrations in particular? Your list will grow rather long as you begin to consider all the things you'd like to know about your future lawyer.

In evaluating him, don't rely on analytical considerations alone; listen to your intuition. Do you like the person? Do you think you could work together creatively as a team in strategy or negotiating sessions? Is he as tough as you'd like? How is he going to come across to the types of people you'll be dealing with? Do you get the feeling that he'll take a genuine interest in your company?

Try to interview the top three or four candidates, even though you may be perfectly happy with the very first one. It's desirable, if only to see some of the range of types available. Additional acquaintances will never hurt you either.

PATENT LAWYERS

Patent law is such a specialized field that even large firms do not ordinarily presume to practice it. When the time comes for a patent lawyer (or if you've come to doubt the abilities of your old one), your attorney can probably supply some valuable leads. Now you will be dealing with an area in which analytical considerations count for much, subjective impressions very little. Here, as in selecting your corporate attorney, however, anything but the best may prove very costly in the long run.

You will be particularly lucky if you can find a top patent lawyer who is already working in or familiar with your particular field. This can save some substantial start-up time and cost. One way of finding such a person is by examining the key patents in your field and contacting the attorneys who wrote them. An out-of-town patent attorney is probably OK since you will not have extensive day-to-day dealings with him, and the dealings you do have can be largely conducted by mail.

In general, just keep in mind: *There's absolutely nothing so expensive as a second-rate lawyer.*

REFERENCES

1 / Vorhees, Theodore, **"Selecting a Lawyer for Your Business"**, in *Management Aids for Small Manufacturers, Annual No. 8.* Washington, D.C.: Small Business Administration, 1962. 66–73.

Practical advice and checklists for any start-up firm.

24

custodial operations and how to avoid them

We trained hard . . . but it seemed that every time we were beginning to form up into teams we would be reorganized. I was to learn later in life that we tend to meet any new situation by reorganizing; and a wonderful method it can be for creating the illusion of progress while producing confusion, inefficiency, and demoralization.

✳   PETRONIUS ARBITER, 210 B.C.   ✳

In applying the principle of enlightened mediocrity to the day-to-day operations of the company, you must be prepared to strike a reasonable balance between custodial and entrepreneurial duties; then let loose of the rest of the custodial chores. This can be a lot harder than it sounds.

At the outset, you were president, operations manager, plant manager, and a lot of other things all rolled up together. The distinctions among these duties were probably not clear because you alone were doing them all at once. As the company evolves, you *must* get rid of many, if not most, of these duties, even if you're convinced that the people to whom you must delegate them can only do a 70 percent job. Your primary energies must be focussed on the *growing edge* of the company— not on the day-to-day struggles. You must be free to press market development and to search for new markets and new products. You must have energy and time for working with new customer prospects, with your financial sources, with government agencies, with possible overseas business contacts. You will need to be looking for possible candidates for acquisition; for key staff members. You must, more than anyone else in your firm, assert to the world your firm's leadership. This involves speaking before technical and business groups, serving on industry and government panels, giving interviews to key publications in your industry, arranging press conferences for new product introduction. You, in short, must be the key, the visible interface between your company and the outside world.

The fact that your time is largely allocated to these presidential duties does not mean that you are any less responsible for the ongoing operation of the firm. It simply means that you must establish the means for *delegation, communication of objectives,* and *feedback on perfor-*

mance—all very elementary Management 101 stuff, you say. However, Management 101 does not tell you how to accomplish this in a tiny company with rapidly changing problems. Moreover, you may have to redefine the jobs, juggle manpower, and rethink your system about every six months for the first couple of years. Things just don't stay neatly in place in the dynamic, sometimes chaotic, atmosphere of the new enterprise.

YOUR ORGANIZATION PLAN

Your delegation (organization) plan should be such that only three or four managers report directly to you. Who they are depends on what business you're in. In general, however, they ought to be:

1 / Financial manager (or chief accountant, controller, treasurer).

2 / Operations manager (or plant manager, office manager, general manager, etc.).

3 / Marketing manager (or sales manager).

4 / Chief engineer (or VP, Engineering, or Technical Director, etc.).

If you have more than about four people reporting to you, you are going to get too involved in custodial management. Some presidents like to have direct reporting from such people as materials manager (purchasing, inventory control, incoming inspection, etc.), or quality assurance manager (quality control, inspection, final test, standards, etc.), personnel manager, and so on. Important though these functions are, to the extent that you become enmeshed in them you will be unable to do your own job.

Following are some general comments on delegating jobs, communicating orders, and eliciting feedback:

✠ FINANCIAL MANAGER

Do not permit this individual to report to anyone but you. The finances of the company are its lifeblood, and you must keep your finger on the pulse. Your financial manager will have a great deal to do, much of which will not require your direct surveillance once the systems are set up to your satisfaction. He will probably function very well with one clerk initially, perhaps adding one more for each additional half-million dollars of volume. The key areas in which you will wish to involve yourself will be:

1 / *Weekly review of cash flow projections and accounts receivable.* A regular 1-hour meeting every week will be sufficient except in times of crisis. This regular schedule will permit your accountant to get his data together and be prepared.

2 / *Preparation of budgets.* This will occur at least every six months, under the general supervision of your financial manager. You will be spending substantial energy at budget time working out all the compromises between programs desired by the operating groups and those permitted by resources available and wrestling with the inevitable conflicts.

3 / *Monthly review of operations, comparing budgeted to actual P&L.* This would typically involve your entire team, including key third-level members with budgetary responsibility. These meetings should occur just as soon after monthly closing as humanly possible—ideally not more than 10 days into the next month. Otherwise, in the general march of events, people tend to forget what went on, and the conditions causing those overruns will still be uncorrected.

Even if you lack an accounting background, make it a point to look over the general ledger, the cash journal, and accounts payable from time to time—unannounced. This will give you an opportunity to spot certain classes of problems, such as late or incorrect posting, jam-ups in certain accounting areas, impending payable and receivable problems, incorrectly computed rep commissions, improper product price entries, etc. More important, it will help to keep your financial manager on his toes. Ask plenty of questions—even though some may be naive.

✠ OPERATIONS MANAGER

You should meet for a couple of hours at least weekly with this gentleman. He will be responsible for many of the major classes of expenditure in the organization, including plant operation, personnel, purchasing, and maybe substantial subcontracting. He will also be responsible for the development and holding of shipping schedules, and the production schedules to back them up. He may also be responsible for the efficient operation of the office, which can be a hard problem in the growing company. In short, he may have more different things to worry about than anybody else in the company.

Your operations manager should be given rather great latitude in the way he does his job. He should be the one to originate requests for labor-saving equipment, design changes to simplify production or procurement, and various cost reduction plans. At the same time, the heat is constantly on him for on-time delivery, acceptable quality, and on-target production costs. He will bear the brunt of many personnel problems and will spend substantial time hiring and training people.

To understand what's happening in his bailiwick, you should try to attend most of his weekly staff meetings (he may call them production status meetings or schedule reviews). This is where the real clashes occur, where tough decisions get made, where incipient ulcers get their start. His meeting is where you find out *why* certain jobs are in trouble, *why* there is a bottleneck in the Test Department. You should not intervene in this sort of meeting, but neither should you isolate yourself from it.

In addition to your weekly meeting with the operations manager, it would be well to spot check, on a non-scheduled basis, the large-dollar areas under his purview. In many manufacturing companies, for example, purchases account for 50–75 percent of all expenditures. It is therefore one of the areas you should probe. Is the buyer doing his whole job, or just struggling to prevent unanticipated parts shortages? Is he getting multiple quotations? Is he maintaining decent vendor records of cost, quality, delivery? Is he actively seeking functional equivalents for high-cost items? Are you engineers getting suggestions and questions from him? Is he the first to raise make-or-buy questions? Is he approaching makers of major purchased items to negotiate annual buys? Is he, in short, initiating action, or just reacting to the press of events? Inventory and stock control are both critical areas in some kinds of operations. Be sure that you look at the inventories and test the methods used to control it from time to time.

Have a look at the phone bills and the invoices for photocopying facilities, etc., occasionally. Remember, you're not being nosey—just interested.

✠ MARKETING MANAGER

You'll have plenty of day-to-day contact with this man in pursuit of specific major orders. However, he should meet with you monthly, and review last month's bookings and the updated forecast for the next quarter. Who are the customers? What are they going to buy, and when? When can we plan to ship? Do this by territory to give yourself some fix on the effectiveness of each rep or salesman. Who is making his quota? How did last month's bookings shape up against forecast? Review the problem areas: contracts lost, customer disputes, salesman problems. What changes in the product are needed? What additional literature? Advertising? Promotion?

The marketing manager must learn sooner or later to accept responsibility for the fact that his forecasts are the basis for all planning for the company. If he is consistently unable to meet reasonable forecasts developed by himself, you may have the wrong man in the job. You must not under any circumstances allow him to isolate you from contact with the customers or the salesmen. You should make it a point to spend at least a quarter of your time with customers and salesmen. If you lose the feel of your market, you've lost touch with the whole business.

✠ CHIEF ENGINEER

If yours is a technology company, the chief engineer should report directly to you. If the emphasis is more on manufacturing and marketing, it may be OK for him to report to the operations manager. In either case, it is incumbent upon you to stay abreast of what's going on in the engineering department. You will want not only a roster of its projects and progress but also some reading on the department's productivity. Engineers are fond of saying, "You can't schedule invention." However true this may be, it is also true that most of what goes on in engineering departments is not invention. It is straightforward application of well-known principles to modify or redesign existing products. You can schedule *and* budget this work, and the chief engineer has the same sort of managerial responsibility for meeting schedule and budget as anybody else on the team.

In the more creative side of his work, is he originating ideas for new products, significant improvements in old ones? Is he a positive force for keeping the company abreast of the state of the art, or is he merely implementing modifications as demanded by the marketing department? Does he provide any ideas for the production and test people? What little R & D projects is he "bootlegging" because he personally believes in them? Does he make it a point to go out and talk to customers once in a while?

Unless your company is heavily involved in innovation, you may not need a scheduled weekly meeting with the chief engineer. However, you should be a presence in the department from time to time to nose around and get a feel for what is (or what is not) happening. And once a month, your chief engineer must be accountable for milestones and budgets, along with everyone else.

TOO MUCH INFORMATION

A basic principle of operation that requires some time for most new presidents to grasp is this: *You should try to learn what the minimum level of information is for you to run the company satisfactorily.* It may be a great deal less than you think. It is literally possible to run certain kinds of companies knowing only the daily cash balance or the day's shipments. The less operational information you personally must process and act on, the better.

There may be certain cases in which you will wish to immerse yourself temporarily in a problem that will require a good deal more information than normal. However, resist the temptation of making the person responsible generate a new report on the problem every month from now on. You won't read them. Handle short-term problems on an *ad hoc* basis, in sufficient depth so that you can actually assist in the solution. Then let your manager see that the agreed-upon solution is implemented, and move on to a different problem. If you try to monitor everything all the time, you will have no time to do presidential work, and you will not contribute very much to the operations either.

It makes us all feel very important to have lots of staff reports, operating statistics, and computer printouts passing over our desks. However, this stuff all costs money to generate, and you should ask in every case: (a) Does this really need my attention, or could somebody else handle it? And (b) Was there any reason for this report at all? What would happen if we eliminated it altogether?

Reports and memos are the basic tools of the empire builders in big companies. In the small company, they can quickly be carried to excess simply because everybody has so much to do anyway. The net cost of being underinformed is probably much less than that of being overinformed.

CONVENTIONAL
WISDOM ⟵ ➡ **REALITY**

You can't know too much about your operation.

There is such a thing as knowing too much about your operation.

REFERENCES

1 / Kelly, P., K. Lawyer, and C. Baumback, *How To Organize and Operate a Small Business* (4th ed.). Englewood Cliffs, N.J.: Prentice-Hall, Inc., 1968.

If you're going to run your company by the book, here's the book to run it by. Covers every phase of small business management, including manufacturing, marketing, accounting, and control.

2 / Thurston, D. B., *Manual for the President of a Growing Company.* Englewood Cliffs, N.J.: Prentice-Hall, Inc., 1962.

This is a big book of practical guidance in a nonexhaustive form. Good treatment of many administrative functions.

3 / Eisenberg, Joseph, *Turnaround Management.* New York: McGraw-Hill Book Co., 1972.

This is an excellent, hard-nosed treatment of many types of business problems, written from a survival point of view. Recommended reading.

4 / Lasser, J. K., *How To Run a Small Business* (3rd ed.). New York: McGraw-Hill Inc., 1963.

5 / Gross, Harry, *Make or Buy.* Englewood Cliffs, N.J.: Prentice-Hall, 1966.

This is a solid treatment of the industrial–engineering viewpoint on make-or-buy decisions.

25

millstones
and
other
fixed
assets

Beware of all enterprises that require new clothes.

❖   HENRY DAVID THOREAU   ❖

THE PERILS OF FIXED ASSETS

There is something uniquely and tangibly gratifying about having a beautiful plant, modern gleaming equipment, and a fully-integrated operation. It is, in a way, a monument to the entrepreneur—a solid testament that *here* is a man who does things first class.

Regrettably, it is often the case that the monument becomes the tombstone of the enterprise. In a study of 95 small Midwest manufacturing firms, Hoad and Rosko [1] observed that only nine were successes. Of the remainder, fully 45 percent of the entrepreneurs felt that unwise investment in capital equipment had been responsible for their failure. Indeed, it is hard to think of a worse use for venture capital than tying it up in bricks, mortar, and machinery. The reasons for this, while obvious, seem to escape a great many entrepreneurs:

1 /   Except in mature firms, the profit arises from sources other than skill in manufacturing. It may be from ingenious product design, proprietary technology, innovative marketing, or just tremendous demand. Very rarely

---

[1] Hoad, William M., and Rosko, Peter, *Management Factors Contributing to Success or Failure of New Small Manufacturers.* Ann Arbor, Mich.: Bureau of Business Research, University of Michigan, 1964.

does it arise because you can make things a lot cheaper than anybody else.

2 / Tying up capital in machinery means there is that much less for product promotion, inventories, accounts receivable, product development, or all the other creative or necessary costs of a growing company.

3 / Committing funds to specialized equipment may be greatly increasing the actual risk of your company. If the product folds, if a better production process is found, or if it's just plain cheaper to buy it elsewhere, you're stuck. You may, to raise cash, be obliged to dump the machinery at a fraction of its cost. If it ties up cash that could otherwise pay creditors, it may be the factor that topples you into bankruptcy.

4 / Apparent cost savings due to improved machinery have a way of being very illusory. They are usually computed on a model of full utilization, long runs, minimal downtime, and other factors that are extremely difficult to guarantee in the fluid environment of a new company or a developing market.

5 / An elaborate plant usually entails costs that are hidden altogether or are hard to evaluate *ex ante*. These include maintenance, power, materials, production scheduling, management time and effort.

Therefore, before committing large amounts of your capital to plant and equipment, weigh carefully the following alternatives:

1 / *Buy the product completely made.* Give somebody else the manufacturing headaches and profit, if any. Contrary to intuition, his price may be substantially lower than your true cost to manufacture simply because he is taking on the work to make a contribution to his existing plant overheads. He may wish to keep workers employed, to keep machines loaded, or to maintain volume with his vendors. For any number of reasons, it often costs *less* to have it made outside. And even if it doesn't, ask yourself if the premuim paid isn't worth it to avoid the extra aggravation and risk of being in manufacturing.

2 / *Buy premade components and simply assemble.* The same arguments apply as in (1), except that you may be less dependent upon a single source. You will be adding value; however, it is likely that you will also be adding to working capital requirements, due to additional inventories of parts and work in process.

3 / *Rent time in someone else's plant.* If your product requires operations on costly machines (e.g., large drop forgings, large injection molded parts, centrifugal castings, etc.), you may be able to find a plant with the requisite machinery willing to sell you machine time, possibly at their marginal cost. Other operations can then be done in your own plant. Computers, circuit testers, environmental test equipment, etc., can also fit this pattern.

4 / *Lease equipment instead of buying it.* This is the final step, short of outright ownership. You may find that the terms of the lease limit your flexibility to a substantial degree, but at least your money is not totally frozen in company-owned plant equipment.

5 / *Consider used or self-constructed equipment.* Depending upon your industry, if a plant seems inevitable, you may be able to find used equipment that will serve the desired purpose for several years, at a fraction of new-equipment cost. If you're looking for machine tools, presses, and other equipment of this sort, there are national listing services to help you locate the desired piece. If it's electronic production or test equipment, computers, simulators, environmental chambers, laboratory equipment, etc., there are innumerable sources for used equipment of this type. Auctions and bankruptcy sales are among the best places to pick up equipment bargains. If the machine is special-purpose, consider the possibility of making it. You may surprise yourself. Give your plant manager a little applause when he *saves* the company $10,000 cash by a little innovation. After all, he deserves it.

All of these routes should receive consideration before buying machinery.

MAKE-OR-BUY ANALYSIS

The usual industrial engineering approach to make-or-buy analysis, while appropriate to large enterprises, may be quite misleading in the small company context. It focuses, predictably, upon the engineering aspects of unit cost. It does not take explicitly into account the overall corporate questions concerning additional financial risk, liquidity, alternate use of capital, and risks of dependence on outside sources. These are likely to be much more significant questions than mere unit cost, but they cannot be properly weighed by your purchasing agent. They are decisions in which you yourself must participate. Similarly, decisions on optimum purchase quantities of materials are often made without adequate attention to the risks of obsolescence, illiquidity, and alternate uses of capital. Long-term supply committments of any magnitude should involve top management, not just the purchasing agent. The apparent savings of volume buying may be dearly bought.

THE PLANT-BUILDING INSTINCT

There are a number of reasons in addition to entrepreneurial ego why companies invest unwisely in plant and equipment. Among these are:

1 / Relative to nonbalance sheet investments (e.g., market development, advertising, which are expensed), plant investment seems somehow "prudent"—after all, it's only changing one asset (money) for another (machinery). The apparent net worth of the company is unaffected.

2 / The plant-building instinct is strong. Your plant manager tends to measure his own worth by the amount of re- sources he can divert into an ever-bigger-and-better plant. Your production engineer will be quick to point out the "savings" and profit improvement that a more efficient plant would produce. Your workers will be quick to take up the cry for better conditions, if it seems to be in the air. Finally, even your financial backers may seem to give tacit plessing to a big new plant. After all, it's a lot more tangible than all that expensed R & D.

3 / There is often a belief, sometimes justifiable, that customers will be impressed by a classy plant, and will therefore be influenced to give you the contract. There is no denying that in some cases this is the decisive factor—especially when dealing with the large company or the government.

For all these reasons, you may find yourself besieged with demands that new plant and equipment be purchased. However, you may be the only person in the company who is in a position to perceive the total effect that this will have on the future of the enterprise as a whole. When you have weighed all benefits, costs, and risks, have the conviction to stick by your decision.

Remember, you will have plenty of other chances to play "You bet your company." Fancy plant equipment certainly is not a high enough pot for that sort of bet.

Parting shot: If you've got $500,000 in the bank, do everything you can to keep it there. The $100,000 cash you save by deferring plant outlays may just be the $100,000 that keeps the company alive next year.

26

life
after death:
our beneficent
bankruptcy
laws

Some days nothing *seems to go right.*

To most of us, the term *bankruptcy* holds connotations comparable to terminal cancer, execution, or just walking off the edge. The bankrupt businessman as social leper is a recurrent American theme. Dark though the connotations may be, however, our liberal laws provide a surprising degree of relief for the bankrupt businessman; indeed, they may be considered as just one more tool of entrepreneurial survival.

WHAT IS BANKRUPTCY?

As generally construed, bankruptcy is the chronic inability to pay one's debts.[1] In the academic sense, it would be defined as having a negative net worth (technical insolvency)—however, many firms operate with negative net worth and are never declared bankrupt by a court. In a

---

[1] Bankruptcy should also be differentiated from *failure*. Dun & Bradstreet defines *five* failure modes: Failed companies cease operation (a) following a bankruptcy or assignment of assets, (b) following an execution, foreclosure, or attachment with loss to creditors, (c) after involvement in court actions involving receivership, reorganization, or arrangement, (d) voluntary withdrawal from business, leaving unpaid obligations, and (e) voluntary compromise with creditors. Note that the company operating under Chapter XI of the Bankruptcy Act of 1938 is *not* a failure in D & B definition.

practical sense, the bankrupt firm is usually characterized by negative working capital (current assets minus current liabilities)—hence the inability to meet current obligations. Indeed, for many entrepreneurs the only thing that differentiates between current conditions and bankruptcy, then, is a state of mind.

The usual causes of bankruptcy are generally a combination of under-capitalization, inept management, and overexpansion. However, there is often a major precipitating factor such as the failure of a large account receivable, a factory fire, a major lawsuit, or the unwillingness of a lender to renew a note. It is uniquely tragic when a company that is growing, even profitably, but absorbing all its cash, is hit by one of these precipitating events. If cash management is poor, the assets are illiquid (e.g., tied up in plant equipment or excessive inventory), or the lending relationships are in poor repair, the result can well be bankruptcy.

WHAT THE LAW SAYS

In ancient Rome, the legal code provided that the bankrupt debtor had to surrender his *person* to the creditor for disposition without any judicial proceeding at all. The creditor could, presumably, put you to work as a slave, or sell you off for that purpose, or possibly donate you for lion-fodder as a wholesome example to other debtors. By the Middle Ages, things had softened a bit, however. Kings could, among other things, grant the bankrupt debtor a delay of payment without consent of creditors.

Colonial America was settled, of course, in significant numbers by debtors released from overcrowded English prisons. However, by 1938 when our present Bankruptcy Act was enacted, society had generally come to recognize that not only is it difficult to obtain further payments from a dead or imprisoned debtor, but it is also very hard to obtain payment from a liquidated or caretaker-managed company. Clearly the debtor has made great progress in the last 2,000 years or so.

The Bankruptcy Act of 1938 provides for the treatment of bankruptcies of many types of enterprises, including utilities, common carriers, financial institutions, and other heavily regulated firms. We are concerned only with two chapters of the Act, however: Chapter X and Chapter XI. In original intent, Chapter X was for application to large, widely held firms, while Chapter XI was intended for small firms with limited claimants. In usage, however, Chapter X has become associated with involuntary bankruptcy, while Chapter XI is usually considered the route of voluntary bankruptcy. Chapter X usually involves the complete removal of the old management, while Chapter XI usually permits it to stay on under a plan of reorganization.

Under Chapter X, either the debtor or three creditors with claims in excess of $5,000 may petition the court for bankruptcy. If the court (a U.S. District Court) grants the petition, it appoints a trustee who takes title of all assets to prevent their dispersion and who submits a plan of reorganization. Two-thirds of the creditors must accept the plan, as well as two-thirds of the stockholders (unless the firm has negative net worth, in which case the stockholders have no say). If the vote fails or if the situation is so bad that there's no hope, in the trustee's view, for recovery of the enterprise, the company is liquidated and creditors paid off according to a priority ranking (with Uncle Sam near the head of the line, of course). A major Chapter X proceeding is a long and costly process, involving fees for trustees, receivers (if appointed), referees, and various experts required perhaps to evaluate the assets and business prospects of the firm. It is made doubly costly by the very good chance that, after the expense of developing a plan, it will be rejected due to the two-thirds vote rule. Chapter X is not a nice experience for anybody but lawyers.

By contrast, Chapter XI can involve fewer steps, fewer people, and fewer costs. The debtor himself usually petitions the court for what the press is fond of calling "protection from creditors". If the petition is granted, the debtor prepares a plan of reorganization which, if accepted by the court, is submitted to the unsecured creditors by a court-appointed referee. Its ratification requires only a majority of the number and dollar claims, and no concurrence whatever from stockholders or secured creditors. If ratified, the court can then make it binding on *all* creditors. While the creditors are considering the plan, they are barred from harassing the debtor who is free to continue running the business. When the plan is approved, he is responsible for its implementation.

Since secured creditors and stockholders have no vote, it is obviously far easier to get a Chapter XI plan approved than it is a Chapter X plan. Moreover, the debtor stays in control of the company throughout. When the plan is finally executed (hopefully), the firm is declared out of bankruptcy. During the life of the plan, however, operations can continue in a reasonably normal fashion; the debtor can even borrow additional funds, allowing lenders preference over the old unsecured creditors.

WHAT'S IN A PLAN OF REORGANIZATION?

The plan of reorganization for a Chapter XI is a little like your financial business plan in that it must convince some very skeptical people of your ability to make the company profitable. This includes, predictably, financial projections, market data, product information, etc. It also includes one other very important item, however: your plan for treatment of creditors. These include, usually, a *reduction* in claim (called "composition of debt"), *extension* of payment date, and often a *substitution* of other securities for debt. Thus, a typical plan of reorganizaiton could offer the following:

1 / To pay off all creditors with claims under $100.

2 / To reduce all other claims to $100 and pay them.

3 / To distribute one share of common stock for each dollar of claims unpaid.

Or you could just resort to the good old 10¢-on-the-dollar method. Or a schedule of payment in full over a long period. Many permutations are possible.

DIVING IN AND DIGGING OUT

Today it looks like the end. The phone never stops ringing, and the creditors aren't just angry—they're starting to panic. You've moved heaven and earth to collect that enormous account receivable, but to no avail— it looks like your customer is going broke and taking you with him. Meanwhile, rumors of creditors' committees have reached your banker, and he's getting nervous, too. The stockholders have started to call up to find out what the hell is going on. The brimstone smell of bankruptcy is in the air. What do you do?

The first thing is this: Don't panic. The second: Get to your attorney fast. If Chapter XI is the only logical route in his judgment, you must waste no time in filing your petition, before the creditors get organized and file theirs for a Chapter X. Once the petition is granted, you have a breathing spell of a week or so to file a plan, and another week or two while the creditors are considering it. During this time you can, of course, work on the problem that sent you into U.S. District Court in the first place, but chances are you won't get it resolved. So keep your fingers crossed, and do whatever you can to persuade holdout creditors that their best chance of recovery is your plan.

Once in Chapter XI, you've got your work cut out. You must make the plan work, or resign yourself to the liquidation of your company. You must function on less cash than ever before. You'll be obliged to cut staff and overheads to the bone; you'll cut advertising, development, and other discretionary costs. You'll need every tactic in the book to operate under the conditions that will prevail (see Chapter 8, under "Operating Without Capital"). You will have to be a veritable Norman Vincent Peale of inspiration and optimism.

There are several groups of people who will require some inspiration and constant attention during this business:

1 / **Customers.** Your customers are your only hope of salvation. Their reaction to the announcement of your bankrupcy will be negative, to say the least. Personally call up or write all customers and visit key customers to explain that the problems are only temporary, that their source of supply is secure, and that you're going to be in business to back up the products they have bought in the past.

Step up your rate of press announcements of new products, new personnel, new anything, to let the world know you're both alive and kicking.

2 / **Creditors.** They are the whole reason for the exercise, and have "donated" a major portion of your new working capital. They deserve to be kept informed. Don't avoid them, be open and cooperative, and continue to try to win their confidence—not just their grudging acquiescence.

3 / **Stockholders.** Even though they had no vote, they are still very important to you. They stand to lose more than anybody; moreover, they may be your only hope of getting additional loans or referrals, so you need them. Send them a monthly memo and let them know how the plan is being pursued.

4 / *Employees and reps.* The last thing you want at this stage is defection of key employees or reps. Keep maximum contact, be a source of inspiration, keep everybody focussed on the tasks at hand, not on the past difficulties. Try sales contests, special incentives, awards for special accomplishment. If you're feeling a trifle gloomy, don't let anybody know it.

If God's willing and the creeks don't rise, you'll dig your way out of Chapter XI. Those who have dug out say it is a uniquely educational experience in hard-nosed management. As a matter of sobering fact, however, it should be noted that fewer than one-tenth of the firms that enter Chapter XI do, in fact, make it out.

Viewed in perspective, Chapter XI is, indeed, a management tool. It permits you to raise working capital by the delightfully simple expedient of stealing it (legally) from your unsecured creditors. Then, with the Court protecting you from their wrath, you're back on the old corner, selling the old goods. Business as usual, except now the stakes have been pushed up a notch: This is your last chance to make it. If you repeat the same mistakes that got you into Chapter XI, you may well expect to end up a Dun and Bradstreet statistic. But even that's a lot better than rowing a galley or nourishing a lion.

A FOOTNOTE ON PENDING LEGISLATION

At time of writing there is before the U.S. Congress a bill to update the 1938 Bankruptcy Act. As written, the bill would create a new Bankruptcy Administration to remove most of the load from the courts and the SEC. Instead of a Chapter X or a Chapter XI, there would be a single, more flexible Chapter VII for all bankruptcies. It would permit debtor-in-possession operations in most cases; however, unlike the totally voluntary Chapter XI, the new law would permit any creditor with a claim of $10,000 or more to force the debtor into reorganization. It would also permit ratification of a plan of reorganization by only a majority of the *claims* (not dollars), making ratification easier to obtain than under either Chapter X or XI at present. Of course, the proposed law contains many other provisions, but all are aimed at the reduction of the time and total cost of bankruptcy proceedings.

REFERENCES

1 / Ma, J. C., and H. D. Henney, "What It Takes To Come Out of Chapter XI", *Credit and Financial Management*, February 1962.

This is a rather interesting article written by a professor and an entrepreneur who have been through it all.

2 / Altman, E. I., *Corporate Bankruptcy in America.* Lexington, Mass.: D. C. Heath Co., 1971.

This is a rather scholarly work, the second half of which is an elaborate model for the prediction of bankruptcy from historical financial data of the firm. However, the first half gives some practical background on present law and practice.

3 / Stanley, D. T., and M. Girth, *Bankruptcy: Problem, Process, Reform.* Washington, D.C.: Brookings Institution, 1971.

This will tell you more than you want to know about bankruptcy law, but it does give some useful insight into the future directions that legislation is likely to take.

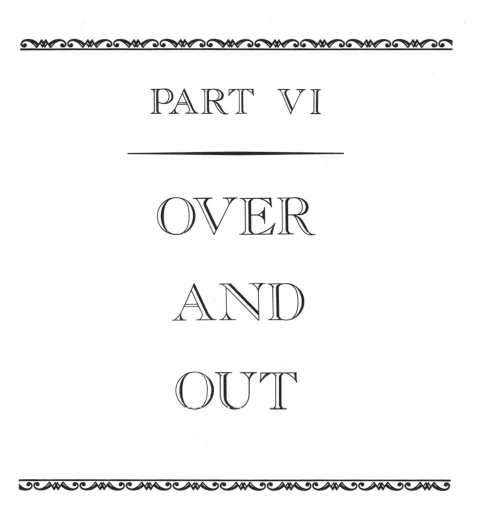

PART VI

OVER AND OUT

27

exit
this
way

Getting into a deal is a cinch, compared to getting out.

❖ ANONYMOUS ❖

WHY GET OUT?

If you're a typical entrepreneur there will come a time when you will want to get out of your company. This is not necessarily just a matter of cashing out, since (a) it is possible that via a secondary issue you have enough cash, and (b) if you liquidated your entire position, you'd have to pay Uncle, then reinvest it someplace else. However, there are several valid reasons why you might very well wish to get out, among which might be:

1 / You have found a better opportunity that you wish to pursue, or you want to look for one.

2 / You're tired/bored with the old business, even if it's successful. You'd like some new problems, some new people, maybe even a new career.

3 / You feel that the major growth phase is over, or possibly you see some serious problems ahead for the company.

4 / You feel that the entrepreneurial phase is over and are not sure of your ability/desire to become the skillful custodial manager needed for the next phase of growth.

For these or a number of other reasons you are statistically likely to be looking for a graceful exit somewhere between 5 and 10 years from start-up.

LIFE STRATEGY

If you're like most of us, a lot more planning goes into your business life than into your personal life. If you need some concrete evidence of this, just look at how irrational your cumulative personal investment decisions seem. The months and years on the firing line of your company make it appear that the company *is* your life. It isn't. It is merely the dominant component in this phase of your life.

It would be well if, one day each year, you would sit down with your husband or wife and update your 10-year plan. This might be very useful, even if it merely serves to identify those areas in which there is no agreement or no possibility of predicting/influencing the outcome. Try setting some goals, just as you do for the business. Remember, a goal differs from a wish. A wish could take the form: "I want to be happy"; a goal would take the form, "By age 45 I wish to retire with a net worth of $750,000." A goal has the characteristics of *concreteness, measurability, time-relatedness,* and *attainability;* in the absence of any of these four characteristics, you don't have a working goal—you have a wish.

Your goals and schedules would include such items as the following:

1 / Acquire physical assets for personal use (e.g., a new home, country place, boat, airplane).

2 / Attain a particular investment goal (e.g., assets of $500,000 yielding unearned income of $25,000 per year).

3 / Change jobs or career.

4 / Travel extensively.

5 / Return to graduate school.

6 / Assume support of parents.

7 / Locate in a desired geographical location.

Your plan must include not only the goals but also the requisite interim steps for getting there, and the milestones that you will establish for measurement of progress toward them. You should also list the risks/obstacles to attainment and the strategies you will employ to overcome them.

To the extent that you are able to integrate the progress of your business into your personal 10-year plan, you will be better able to make correct decisions about whether, when, and how to exit from the company. In fact, it will pull many other elements of your personal decision making into focus as well.

EXIT MODES

There are several exit modes from the company. These include, mainly:

1 / Business failure.

2 / Getting fired by directors.

3 / Selling to another firm.

4 / Selling your stock to private parties, including others in the company.

5 / Selling your stock in a public secondary offering.

Not all will be available to every entrepreneur, obviously. They differ in rate of personal exit, rate of financial exit, and range of follow-on options.

✠ BUSINESS FAILURE

When the doors are closed involuntarily, it is usually the end of the road for the firm, but not necessarily for the entrepreneur. He's usually out looking for a new deal the next morning, although the failure of his last one may take some tall explaining. Some ultra-entrepreneurial types have even been known to show up at their firm's liquidation auction, buy up the assets at 5¢ on the dollar, and behold: They are back on the old corner Monday morning.

The folding of your company, however, may provide an appropriate juncture to pause and reflect. Was it really bad luck, or are you yourself weak in certain areas that may jeopardize success in future ventures? What lessons can be gleaned from the experience? Try writing yourself an essay on the experience, complete with prescriptions for dealing with the forces that led to your last company's downfall.

✠ GETTING FIRED BY DIRECTORS

This is, in some respects, more undesirable than business failure, although it is possible that it leaves you with more assets, therefore more options as to future action. Again, some careful analysis of yourself and your company's history is in order to establish precisely what went wrong and how to avoid a repeat performance. Be honest. Was it bad management, bad people, or bad luck?

✠ SELLING TO ANOTHER FIRM

This exit route, among the most common for entrepreneurs, is not necessarily an exit at all. In selling your company, it may also be necessary to sell yourself for a number of years since without you the value of the enterprise may be much lower, and the acquiring firm knows it. This is especially true if the selling company is to be operated as a subsidiary. It is perhaps less true if you are to become a division or a department.

The new role may be bondage or a fantastic opportunity, depending upon circumstances and your state of mind. Many companies look to their subsidiary acquisitions as a major source of future top executives, as well as of growth and diversification for the parent. Others see the acquisition as a sort of portfolio investment, a part of which is the entrepreneur. He is bought with it and sold with it, as circumstances demand.

The situations of acquired executives vary widely. Some are locked in only for a given time period; others are locked in by a stock workout arrangement that bases stock price on subsidiary performance. Some are given great latitude—for example, in acquiring other firms. Others are kept on a very short tether, indeed.

If your firm was originally financed by a large corporation, or its venture capital subsidiary, you probably have no choice as to whom to sell. In fact, the pricing formula may already exist. If this is not the case, however, selecting a corporate partner can require some serious research. If, as in the case discussed in Chapter 25, you are headed for calamity, you probably haven't much leisure in which to check out the fine points. If this is not the case, however, you should review your prospective bedfellow rather carefully. Before approaching anybody, you should develop a list of criteria to aid you, your directors, and perhaps a consultant in the search for appropriate corporate partners. These criteria could, for example, include:

1 / Size of company.

2 / Present business.

3 / Experience in acquisitions. Are they sophisticated, or will they make all their mistakes with you? Will you get a better price from an unsophisticated firm?

4 / Familiarity with your industry and market.

5 / Availability of resources needed by your company (e.g., manufacturing capacity, marketing ability, raw materials, working capital).

6 / Geographical location. There are pros and cons to close proximity to one's corporate parent.

7 / General progressiveness. While a progressive partner may normally be desirable, sometimes the presence of some new blood is what a company needs to revitalize it, creating a bigger opportunity for the new blood.

8 / Ownership status. Is it on the NYSE, OTC, or privately held? What is the stability of its stock?

9 / Character and reputation of management.

You will be able to think of several dozen more criteria. You should rank or weight them before putting them to use. Remember, even a bad set of criteria is better than simply selling out on the basis of willingness of the other firm to buy. Your choice should, of course, be heavily influenced by your personal 10-year-plan since you may in effect be making a long-term career choice at the same time.

✠ Selling Your Stock to Private Parties

Such a route may be available to you on favorable terms. However, even more than the acquiring corporation, the buyers are likely to need you to run the company for some substantial period of time. To ensure this, they may be willing to offer attractive bonuses, option plans, or other incentives to keep you on board.

A major exception, of course, is the case in which your partners and/or stockholders are buying you out to get rid of you. Your greatest obstacle to rational action at this point may be the involvement of your own ego in the process. If the other members of the team are inalterably opposed to your leadership, it may be best for you, too, if you bow out. You are going to have nothing but trouble from now on if you stay. A fight for the sake of winning may ensure that *everyone* loses out.

The toughest problem at this juncture is in getting a fair price for your stock. If it develops that you can't, consider leaving *with* the stock, and let them figure out how to increase its value. A partial solution of some stock and some cash may be the most equitable.

✠ SELLING YOUR STOCK IN A PUBLIC SECONDARY OFFERING

This is without a doubt the route that has made more millionaires out of entrepreneurs than any other. Subject to timing in the business cycle and other factors, the public has historically been willing to pay more for stock in a growing company than anybody. While an acquiring corporation might be willing to pay 10 times earnings, or perhaps its own price–earnings ratio, the public may pay 50 times, 100 times, or maybe infinity times earnings. There is no guarantee of this, however, and there are many more risks and hazards than in private acquisition. For example, if your initial public offering (in which you cannot sell any of your personal stock) comes out at 20, and the market promptly takes a nose dive, leaving you at 10, it may be all but impossible to get a secondary offering out. Too many people have already lost money on your stock.

Your ability to pull off a satisfactory secondary offering may also be related to the investment banker who handles your offerings. Assuming that company performance is satisfactory, your secondary offering success may depend upon whom your investment banker sold the initial offering to, at what price, and how much support (i.e., buying for his own account in times of market weakness) he has given the stock. If your stock price has risen a bit and held up well, you're golden. If it's fallen a bit and stuck there, you're in for a long wait.

Selection of an investment banker deserves about the same amount of energy as selection of a corporate partner since, in the best case, he *is* a corporate partner. The worst kind takes a firm public, then disappears. The best hang on through good and bad, and try to ensure that each successive public offering sets the stage for the next.

In establishing your list of criteria for an investment banker, you may need a little help since this is a world with which few entrepreneurs are familiar. You may wish to enlist your banker, lawyer, or accounting firm on the job. Among the possible criteria are:

> *1 /* Familiarity with initial offerings of smaller companies. The largest, most prestigious house may strike out completely in this department.

2 / Success with small-company offerings. Their score is a matter of public record. Moreover, presidents of their client firms are readily identified for further checks. Look at the record. What happened to their deal?

3 / "General reputation" in the financial community. This is a vague parameter, but one that will profoundly affect their ability to sell out your issue quickly. Ask several people, including your attorney and directors, to rank a list of 20 firms you give them. Try the same thing on your broker and your banker. A pattern may begin to emerge.

4 / Present types of issues. Just because they have done your kind of offering in the past is no guarantee they would do it or do it well today. Was there a specific champion in the house who is no longer there? Where did *he* go?

5 / Your intuitive reaction. Does the guy come on like a big-time hustler, a torpid old aristocrat, or a reasonable fellow with whom you can discuss your business problems? Be sure it's somebody you can personally like and trust.

The selection and dealing with investment bankers is a realm where war stories abound. It may be constructive to listen to a few, and there is no better source than an entrepreneur who has just gone through it. Seek out a couple and see what they have to say.

Initial offerings, except in the case of *very* strong issuing companies, are seldom underwritten (i.e., they are normally taken on in a best-efforts mode by the underwriter). If he is unable to sell an agreed-upon minimum (e.g., 80 percent of the issue), you both simply walk away from the agreement. Such an agreement usually involves a hefty fee for the investment banker if he's successful (say, 10 percent of the offering), plus some warrants or cheap stock for his own portfolio. This latter is very important since it creates an incentive for him to support your stock and also to promote favorable conditions for a secondary offering so that he can cash in.

When you and an investment banker have agreed to work together, there will ensue a negotiation of the different variables of the offering: percent of ownership, pricing, timing, compensation to investment banker, and other considerations. There will be the question of expenses to be picked up by each side, of the retention of special counsel (often of the investment banker's choice) for SEC work, and many other considerations. These are all very critical areas that may have a profound effect on the company's fortunes and your personal net worth. Your attorney should, of course, be a party to this negotiation. Try to be cooperative without being a patsy. If you honestly feel that they are trying to dictate unreasonable terms, say so. There are other investment bankers; it isn't the end of the world if talks are terminated.

A note on expense is in order. In addition to the investment banker's commission, your company will be expected to pick up the bills for legal, audit, and SEC registration work incident to the offering. For an offering of, say, $2 million, this could be as much as $50,000. This is bad enough if the offering goes well. It may be disaster for the company, however, if for some reason the offering doesn't sell. Thus, the public offering must be undertaken with an appreciation of this risk, and with a contingency plan of recovery if the worst happens. Do not let the euphoria of public issue and mushrooming paper net worth cause you to lose sight of this very real hazard.

A FINAL NOTE ON GETTING OUT

Your 10-year plan will give you some guidance as to whether, how fast, and how completely you should get out of your firm. Market conditions and the progress of the company itself will provide constraints. However, some things must be experienced to be understood. This is particularly true of being at loose ends with a lot of money.

The folklore is full of stories about entrepreneurs who cashed out, intending to retire with a bundle, only to discover after six months of walking the beaches that they *really* only wanted to start another company. Most of these stories are probably true. The personality traits, drives, and abilities that made you an entrepreneur in the first place do not go away the day you cash out. They are part of your permanent software. Therefore, don't be surprised if your game plan to retire at 40 must be extensively revised when you reach the goal. This will be a happy result for everyone if it happens because it means that a decision has been reached to put back in use one of society's most valuable assets: a successful entrepreneur!

REFERENCES

1 / Strange, M., ed., *Acquisition and Merger Negotiating Strategy.* New York: Hawthorne Books, Inc., 1971.

This book, written from the viewpoint of the acquiring firm, will offer you some insights on how to be acquired on the most advantageous terms.

2 / O'Neal, F. H., *Expulsion or Oppression of Business Associates— Squeeze-Outs in Small Enterprises.* Durham, N.C.: Duke University Press, 1961.

This rather academic book reviews virtually all squeeze-out techniques in general use, and examines some of the remedies of the squeezee. Required reading!

INDEX